Me in the Making

One Man's Journey To Becoming A School Superintendent

Me
in the
Making

One Man's Journey To Becoming A School Superintendent

Dr. Walter Milton, Jr.

One-L Group

Published by
One-L Group
P.O. Box 9095
Springfield, IL 62791-9095

Published in the United States

ISBN 978-0-615-32325-1

Cover design by Ebony L. Stith

Dedication

This book is dedicated to my father, the late Walter Milton, Sr., who made his transition as this book was going to print.
These words truly express what my dad meant to me.
His spirit will always be a part of my life, lifting me, comforting me and guiding my every movement.

Forty-One Years of Guidance

You guided me from my first breath to the day
that you departed this world.
Other than God, you reigned supreme.
My mother taught me love and patience; you, my father, taught
me responsibility, a work ethic and how to be a man.
I must say, with the two of you, I have been heavenly blessed.
I remember the times you held my hand and protected me from
the elements of life that challenge the spirit of a young man.
You guided me through winds and storms of my life's journey by
reminding me that I can make it through if I
"just ask God to direct my path."
You reminded me that I was a king,
every time that I fell from my throne.

You modeled perseverance and
you assured me that you would never leave me.
You stayed and I am forever thankful.
You inspired me to live a life of honesty, integrity, love,
humility and commitment.
I am grateful that I earned your approval.
You taught me trust, because you freely and creatively allowed me
to depend on you and you never let me down.
I have reaped the benefits of your sacrifice;
now the baton has been passed.
I intend to do the same and will strive to be a strong father to my
children as you were to me.
As you always told me, no matter what,
never forsake your children!
I intend to make the sacrifice.
Forty-One Years of Guidance that will last me for a lifetime.
Although you may not be present in the physical world,
your spirit lives in me, my sons and their sons to be,
so on and thereafter.
Through your guidance, I am you as you are me.
One love, we live on forever!

Acknowledgements

First and foremost, I thank God for the gift of family and their
unyielding patience and support. My parents for giving me my
wings to soar; my wife, Lisa, for her unconditional love and
creating a home environment where I am free to be me.
It is impossible to travel life's journey without cheerleaders along
the way. I have been very fortunate to have had in my life, and
still have, many wonderful cheerleaders and nurturers to help me
navigate life's curves and sometimes roadblocks. There are too
many to name, but they know who they are. I say "thank you"
for being able to give me exactly
what I needed when I needed it.
I would like to give a special "thank you" to my editor and friend
for her countless hours of content review and rewrites. This book
would not have been possible without her support and commitment to this project. In addition, although I have had many
nurturers, I would be remiss if I do not publicly acknowledge Dr.
T.C. Wallace for his years of friendship and mentoring. His
insights into the field
of education are invaluable.
I am reminded of the song writer's words, "I don't feel no ways
tired because He has brought me too far to leave me!" Thank
you, Father Mother God Spirit; Your Grace and Mercy still carry

me through. Peace, blessings and love to
all of you who paved the way,
smoothed my path and hydrated my soul to make my journey
all that it has been!

Ten Guiding Principles for Highly Effective Preschool-Grade 12 Learning Communities

1

Every "human life" must be viewed as important, unique, special, different and wonderful.

2

Children have an inalienable right to learn and grow in a well-structured formal educational program that is systematic, standards and research based, safe, healthy, engaging, and guided by highly qualified and competent staff.

3

Consistent consideration of the differentiated learning styles and needs of students is the linchpin of successful instructional programs.

4

All children are natural learners who learn best through sensory-discovery and numerous opportunities for inquiry, exploration, investigation and engagement of complex thinking skills.

5

All academic achievement is the result of language acquisition and reading proficiency in four core learning areas: English Language Arts, Math, Science, and Social Studies.

6

Life success is equally the result of a positive self-concept and intellectual acuity.

7

Parents are the most important teachers and must be included in the educational process of their children.

8

School educators are the most significant teachers and must participate in ongoing sustained training that continuously builds skills in the latest milestones in teaching and learning.

9

Local and national community involvement is crucial for establishing expectations of excellence for children and youth.

10

Every "human life" has the right to reach their maximum potential.

"Me in the Making, is a remarkably refreshing and honest story of courage, disappointment, and courage again".

Rick Miller, Founder
Kids at Hope
Phoenix, AZ

"Me in the Making" left me with a stronger feeling of hope for today's youth in school systems nationally. Fatherhood played an important role along with his desire and passion to positively affect today's educational policies and practices. I applaud Dr. Milton for his honesty and ability to share his personal and professional experiences with the world".

Sam McNabb, Founder/President
Seado Enterprises, Inc. &
The National Football Players Father Association
Riverdale, IL

Contents

Prologue

"I only have a minute. Only sixty seconds in it. Forced upon me--can't refuse it. Didn't seek it, didn't choose it. But it's up to me to use it. I must suffer if I loose it. Give an account if I abuse it. Just a tiny little minute. But eternity is in it."
--Benjamin E. Mays

According to predictions, expectations, and assumptions of others, my life's journey should not have become my today's reality. Unfortunately, there were scores of people who told me that I could not accomplish my goal of becoming a school superintendent by age thirty-five. You see, historically, the norm has been that only older men as superintendents were capable of steering the education of the nation's children. However, through what I call divine intervention and hard work, I became superintendent right on target according to my goals and aspirations.

Although this book is from an educational construct, it is also designed to inspire and provide the reader with a clear understanding of the importance of having definitive goals, undying faith, confidence and humility. Life offers an array of richness, yet in order to sample its riches, one must have the knowledge to realize the importance of mastering one's craft. Although I did not have material riches, the experiences of my formative years were wealthy. The principle of maintaining my focus was presented to me early in my life as a part of my conservative upbringing. My parents understood that for me education was a matter of life and death - it was the great equalizer.

There are many facets of my professional life that are quite unique, which may instruct or inspire others. And while this is my story, I am most certain that many will find similarities. Giving of one's self to help another is truly an indisputable gift.

I began my educational career as a teacher in two suburban school districts, after which I became an administrator in an urban district. I have even spent time teaching in a private school. My first superintendent opportunity was in a rural district. Currently, I am a newly appointed superintendent in an urban district with somewhat of a "suburban flair." These experiences have proven invaluable on my journey in that it is very rare for an educator to have had experiences in districts with completely different dynamics.

I am a pioneer in that I was the first African American superintendent in two of the school districts, and also the youngest in all of the districts in which I served, and am currently serving. It is worthy to mention, too, that I was the first African American male to teach in two New York suburban districts. Throughout these different experiences, there remains one constant: I have discovered that all children are beautiful, different and have potential for greatness in spite of their circumstances. I learned not to see where they are currently, but to see what they can become. As a young child, I had the great fortune of someone seeing my possibilities and potential greatness.

I knew that in order for me to bring about change in the educational arena, I would become a superintendent. This interest was sparked from experiences I had in both high school and college. Another reason for wanting to become a school superintendent was, and still is, my love for children. Indeed, I am passionate about the art of teaching and learning. As a superintendent, I am able to assist in development and implementation of policy and analyze the results. Educating our children is serious business and not a joking matter! Again, education is a matter of life and death. The awesome task of an educator is to teach not only to the cognitive-self but the social-self, the emotional-self, the physical-self, the linguistic-self and the spiritual-self. Unfortunately, many children arrive at school every day with broken spirits. Proverbs: 18:14 (NKJV) states "The spirit of a man will sustain him in sickness, but who can bear a broken spirit?"

Being a school superintendent is often times a thankless job. It is not a glamorous position; it has many challenges, disappointments and moments of sheer loneliness. It is the only job on earth in which continued employment is contingent on not ruffling feathers. The more aggressive the approach in school reform can sometimes severely impact a superintendent's career. However, superintendency also has its share of rewards, especially when one can create an environment where children are achieving. This kind of leadership requires that one is willing to make tough decisions based on what is best for children, and that may conflict with the agendas of the adults to whom those children are entrusted.

I strongly believe that American society, in general, encourages and appreciates the value of a quality education. It has certainly been widely accepted that education is a vital tool necessary to create and sustain a thriving and forward-moving citizenry. In other words, our children's education must be secured and protected. I also strongly believe that all children are capable of learning, as I am a product of this form of thinking. I have dedicated my life to finding the means to make sure that all children take advantage of the opportunities to learn.

My first district in which I served as superintendent was Fallsburg Central School District, located in the southeastern part of New York State, approximately an hour outside of downtown Manhattan. Fallsburg was small by national educational standards, approximately 1400 students K-12. In retrospect, this was quite a significant accomplishment, for I became a school superintendent after leaving the principalship of a middle school in the heart of the urban community in upstate New York. I really enjoyed being a principal; in fact, I truly treasure all of my professional educational experiences, especially classroom teaching. I believe that the best school administrators are the ones who remain teachers at heart. One common thread I will carry throughout all of my experiences is that I know my purpose is to affect the lives of children in a meaningful way.

People are not always receptive to change. Some believe that certain pathways must be followed to garner achievement. Experience has taught me that there is always more than one route to reach a destination. Taking a deep breath and making your own path, though sometimes more arduous and daunting, is certainly worthwhile in the end. I never embrace doubt or give in to the spirit of un-readiness in any of my endeavors. If one has the knowledge, tenacity, ability to communicate clearly, and knows how to build relationships and draw upon outside support and resources, the chances for positive outcomes are on the horizon. Life provides numerous opportunities; one must remain open to receive and to take full advantage of them. I am a testament to defying the odds and breaking down barriers.

If I had listened to all of the naysayers, although I do realize that they were speaking from the context of their experiences, I probably would have remained a principal, fighting feverishly to find a position in central administration somewhere in the United States. I identified some personal skill building goals throughout my career to prepare myself for school superintendency. Being a visionary is critical; one must assemble and remain steadfast to his or her vision regardless of adversity or triumph. Again, be mindful not to absorb doubt or negative energy from others. You must have internal mechanisms in place that reject such forces and keep you positively focused at all times.

It is important to recognize and accept that the path to any position of executive leadership can be a very lonely place; therefore, establishing and maintaining relationships based on trust and honesty are paramount. Nurturing relationships can sustain you during times of turmoil.

Years ago, Norman Vincent Peale introduced the Power of Positive Thinking, a principle that can be the foundation for anyone's success, our thoughts drive our actions and experiences. My mother always said "the human mind is a powerful instrument." Understandably, it is imperative to program your mind to be goal-oriented and to concentrate on achieving those goals.

Other than God, I attribute a great deal of my success to the philosophical framework known as my *Guiding Principles for Educational Greatness As They Relate To Effective Leader-*

ship. These principles describe my core beliefs and value system relative to leadership. I share these principles with you because I believe that the greatest gift one can receive is the responsibility of leadership, and true leadership is having the ability to serve others.

Effective Leadership

- Follow an unwavering code of honesty and ethical conduct. Speak out against unfairness, injustice, and corruption, regardless of who may be guilty

- Have the ability to bring together previously conflicting factions to create a stronger, unified body

- Appeal to the masses of people and not just those of the elite class or leadership hierarchy

- Propose specific solutions to problems as opposed to vague philosophical concepts

- Consistently represent the desires and concerns of the people and speak or negotiate on their behalf

- Seek opinions and advice from followers before making major decisions

- Support positive programs even in the absence of public recognition or personal financial gain

•Demonstrate humility and understanding that leadership is a responsibility given by others and not an opportunity for self-aggrandizement

•Delegate responsibility to competent people, teach them to assume leadership, and prepare for an orderly transition of authority upon the end of the leader's term of service.

A superintendent's role brings with it excitement, anticipation and the opportunity to learn. Most importantly, it provides one with the chance to shape and mold young lives. I have learned through successes and challenges that past experiences can have little to do with one's current superintendency. Each district demands its own unique set of tools. Additionally, American culture differs depending on the region of the country and the school district.

It is my hope that you find this reading interesting, informative, and inspirational. Since I am an educator, I feel it necessary to also provide information that is research based. I will share with you some of my experiences that have prepared me for where I am today. Perhaps there is information and ideas that may be useful and worthwhile to you. There are many people throughout history who have amazing stories of perseverance; I take this opportunity to introduce you to my story.

Included in the last section of this book are copies of my Superintendent's Entry Plan, which can be a useful tool for anyone pursuing a leadership role within **any** organization; Six Essentials for Highly Effective Schools; a Literature Review on Parent Involvement that I have written, along with a host of additional references.

Chapter One

Believe In Yourself:

The Journey Begins

"My parents always instilled in me to believe in myself."
-Me

Every Reader can find themselves throughout these pages. Different content however, it is the same context. No matter what our experiences are we all have a self - discovery and if we are fortunate, we learn something along the way.

I remember entering school at an early age trying to determine where I belonged. I grew up in a large family, especially by today's standards; I had six sisters and one brother. Family, both immediate and extended, has always played an important role in my life. In the midst of my second and third years as a Superintendent, eight deaths occurred in my family over an 11-month period. I lost an aunt, uncle, four cousins, a sister and a brother. After the loss of my sister and brother, I experienced grief; however, I knew that I had to persevere and continue to lead in a manner that was efficient and responsible. From these experiences I have learned to manage people and situations withoutnegativity, foolishness and mistrust. When a person has been affected by a series of deaths, his or her life's view changes. He or she often finds joy simply in the pursuit of helping others.

The importance of a quality education was stressed in my household and I took that expectation seriously. My parents truly led by example; both of them will always remain the two hardest working people that I have ever known.

My father was the driving force in my life as it relates to work ethic, commitment, perseverance, and honoring responsibilities as a man. He held true to the notion that responsibility is not an emotion, it is a commitment. Responsible people are those who do what needs to be done regardless of the circumstances. My father has been a pillar in my life, and I am devoted to leaving the same legacy for my children. He once told me that "sometimes a home without a father is like a house without a roof": potentially the home can not weather the many storms that come. My father was a giant in my life. The countless memories of the moments my father and I shared will always be cherished.

My father spent a great deal of time sharing insight of challenges that would come my way as I matured toward manhood. Often times fathers do not realize the importance of sharing their life's experiences with their children. My father talked about his life in a way that it seemed as though I went back in a time machine. His stories were vivid. He told me of the struggles he endured growing up in South Carolina and the level of contempt that black men faced on a daily basis. He always told me to take seriously the struggles of those before me.

I remember as a little boy, no more than four years old, when my father took me along with him to the Carolinas to visit relatives. I remember him placing me on the lap of my great-grandfather who was from the islands. My great-grand father was in the beginning stages of going blind. I remember touching his skin that was as smooth and thick as refined leather. He rubbed my head and smiled continuously. The experience seemed like an eternity. My father revered his grandfather and his father. My father told me that it was important that my great grandfather met me before he died. He shared with me that my great grandfather said that I was a special addition of patriarchs in the Milton lineage. My great grandfather lived to be well over one hundred years. I was exposed to strong men all of my life. Men who valued their families, were great providers, were humble and most importantly, who loved through their actions.

My mother exemplifies a woman of high moral standards and wisdom. She taught me many lessons through her patience and love, all the while instilling in me an undying love for self, culture and others. Mom always told me that I can be anything that I wanted to be if I dedicated myself and believed in myself. My mother and I have a bond that will never be broken. I have learned how to love my wife as a result of loving my mother.

As a child I struggled with guilt. I felt guilty over the smallest things; I shared this problem with my mother, and like most good mothers, she already knew my issue. One day she sat me down, handed me this beautiful shiny stone, and said "if you carry this little stone with you everyday and everywhere you go, you will not experience guilt." Like any child, I believed wholeheartedly the words she spoke. For weeks I carried this little stone in my pocket. I was confident in my actions; I did not second guess my decisions and guilt did not get the best of me. Then one day something strange happened, I lost the stone. I became frantic and immediately reverted to the thoughts and feelings of guilt. I shared the occurrence with the woman whom I loved and trusted the most. Mom explained to me in her loving calm demeanor that it was not the stone that served as the tool of liberation, it was my mind. She told me that she had taken the stone because it was time for me to realize that I had the power within me. That valuable lesson will remain with me for the rest of my life.

When I began high school in Rochester, New York, the home of Kodak, Xerox, Bausch & Lomb and other major corporations, I often witnessed many of my peers striving to graduate from high school with the only focus of graduating and getting a "good job." My entire neighborhood held this sentiment/value. College was seen as something out of the realm of possibility and in other cases unnecessary. Gratefully, my parents instilled in me the importance of college. It was never a question of if I were going to college; it was always where I would be attending. My best friend, Myron Lester, and I were determined to break the mold and not only attend college, but graduate. We spent hours discussing our goals and aspirations. Unfortunately, we witnessed too many of our peers dying or being incarcerated for drugs or violent crimes. However, our parents encouraged us to excel academically and use education as the key to success.

My quest for a quality education for all children began early in my life. I vividly remember sitting in my elementary classes and, at certain times, feeling invisible. I realized the state of invisibility would only dissipate if I acted out. In many cases I found that whenever I succumbed to peer pressure, it only served as a form of immediate gratification. I also reminded myself that I had parents at home who took my education seriously; simply put, I was too afraid of the consequences if I allowed myself to be characterized as a disruptive student. Deep down inside I wanted desperately to be recognized as a student who had attributes that were meaningful and constructive. I know there are scores of young people who feel just as I did. They struggle with these same issues on a daily basis. My parents made sure I knew that education was the great equalizer to compete in a system that historically denied equal access for African Americans.

My high school experience was somewhat different. I became an incredible athlete, and excelled on the football field. I was recognized as an outstanding quarterback for my high school team for four years (I played varsity football for those years). Although I was compelled to play in college, which I did, I knew that football alone was not going to enable me to achieve academically. I knew that it was imperative that I concentrated on academics.

I had supportive teachers in high school that displayed love and shared the gift of knowledge. Two teachers in particular, who stood out, were my ninth grade science teacher and my high school social studies teacher. They taught me that effective teaching is not a vocation, it is a devotion. Effective teachers are committed to addressing the needs of their students. I decided, while sitting in my ninth grade science class that I wanted to become an educator. If someone could profoundly impact my life the way they did, it was necessary for me to do the same for others. These two teachers consistently told us about the opportunities available if we made education a priority. Overall, they were truly role models, developing students who were allowed to dream.

A strong classroom ethos that supports high student achievement drives for a shared mission, vision, and set of core beliefs. Without this foundation, best efforts are derailed by confusion, lack of direction, and fragmentation. Having high expectations for children is vital. Children have a unique way in which they work diligently to meet high expectations if they feel safe, secure and loved. It has always been my desire to inculcate the following regardless of my position; develop students that:

1.   Are self-directed learners
Self-directed learners have the qualities and skills to direct their own learning in a variety of settings. Learning will not always be in a formal setting and students will need to condition themselves to prepare for their future.

2.   Have high self esteem
A positive self image is extremely important as attitude and confidence enable one to persevere while working towards accomplishing their goals. The belief in self has to be a prerequisite for students. I often share the words of a poem/mantra I learned in undergraduate school while pledging for a fraternal organization, Phi Beta Sigma with students. These words have inspired me throughout my daily vicissitudes, they are powerful, and they are as follows:

Believe in Yourself!

Don't give up the fight; just keep struggling with all of your might, resolve that you will not yield in despair, your burdens then become lighter to bear.

Believe in Yourself!

Work doubly hard to achieve your goals despite every odd, the faith in oneself and the will to succeed are the prerequisites that all of us need.

Believe in Yourself

And be not dismayed, but take courage in those who have made the grade, just keep moving with a resolute will and you will reach the top of life's rugged hills.

Believe in Yourself!

3.   Demonstrate RESPECT for self and others, and accept responsibility for their actions

Students need to value the importance of accepting responsibility for their actions and understanding they are in control of the choices they make. Having respect for self, others and property are vital aspects of the socialization process.

4.   Exemplify the following attributes

•Ability to effectively communicate orally or in written format

•Ability to work with a group to successfully accomplish tasks and achieve goals

•Ability to problem solve within personal, professional and social environments and experiences

• Ability to think critically and analytically
• Ability to develop an effective decision making process
• Ability to establish clear goals and objectives

5.   Demonstrate that they can think and learn for understanding

Prepare students to develop the academic knowledge and skills which will assist them to retain and apply their knowledge. Understanding facts, skills (processes) and concepts within a specific discipline is necessary to be productive and efficient in that area.

One of the most sacred things that my parents taught me was that realizing dreams requires a plan. You must prepare, work hard and stay focused. Happiness is when dreams come to fruition with a foundation of loving, being loved and successfully raising a family. Our children need to be reminded through our words and our actions that they are loved and honored.

Family is the cornerstone of my existence. I thank God every day for blessing me with the richness, peace and love that my family provides. I remind those who are close to me how much they really mean to me, and how much I treasure the moments we share. Love is the most powerful emotion in the universe and many of us lose sight of it.

As educators and parents, we must consistently feed the spirits of our children with love, greatness and excellence and remind them that they can accomplish whatever they desire. Believing in our children is the impetus to them believing in themselves. Hard work, undying faith and the ability to dream freely are the keys to goal accomplishment. There are many young people who do not reach their true potential, because somewhere along the way they were hindered and distracted from their dreams.

Prior to becoming an administrator, I taught for five years. I learned that effective teachers have the ability to enhance students' learning in a rich, creative and enthusiastic way. In order to gain intellectual growth, it is imperative to provide an environment where students feel safe, engaged and challenged. Engaging students was important to me. As a classroom teacher, my goal was to teach my students to become critical and analytical thinkers with a social conscience. Each child I have been blessed to serve is like a beautiful flower.

The best school administrators remain teachers at heart, whether they are coaching teachers to become more effective in the classroom or assisting other administrators in strengthening their instructional leadership skills.

In retrospect, I had a somewhat unique introduction to the world of teaching and administration. As I previously stated, I knew that I wanted to become a classroom teacher in the ninth grade and an administrator/superintendent in my junior year of college after completing a New York State Minority Public Policy internship. My goals were definitive and clear early on in my life. Most importantly, though, I believed in myself.

Chapter Two

My Roadmap

"Everyone is more or less the master of his own fate."
-Aesop from "The Traveler and Fortune"

Becoming a school superintendent is the main product here, but you can find lessons in any process or path that you decide to take. I find it imperative that one has a plan and work their plan to the best of their ability. Although your plan may experience challenging moments, I encourage you to remain on your path.

I launched my campaign to seek employment in education after completing my master's degree and obtaining my secondary teaching certification. I was a young single father with a son born during my sophomore year in college. I was able to graduate even under these circumstances with the help and support of my family. I vowed that my son and I would not become another "black male"

statistic. Landing my first teaching position was not without challenges. However, I was hired as a football coach in a district in
which I did not initially apply. I applied in the Rochester City School
District, the urban district from which I graduated. I waited and
waited to hear the news that I had been hired by the district where I
felt so familiar, but the news never came. As the new school year
approached, my concern turned to confusion in that I knew most
school districts supposedly were seeking to hire young, African
American males. To my dismay, my beloved Rochester City School
District never contacted me. In retrospect, my career may have
taken a different path had I begun teaching in Rochester at that time.
Every event has a purpose.

Returning to my apartment from coaching football one
hot and muggy August evening, I began to contemplate my next
strategies to land a position in the Rochester City School District.
I knew that I had a great deal to offer students and I was relentless
in my efforts to bring this to fruition. Substitute teaching was not
an option for me; I had this experience while in graduate school.
Wondering about the outcome in terms of landing a teaching
contract in the district which I so dearly desired, my contempla-
tion was interrupted by a phone call. The caller was an administrator in the district in which I had received the opportunity to
coach high school football. He shared with me a conversation he
had with one of the district's principals. He indicated that the
principal had received almost three hundred applications for an
open eighth grade social studies position. However, he was not
extremely pleased with the applicants interviewed thus far. The
administrator asked the principal if the name Walter Milton, Jr.,
rang a bell; the principal said "no." The principal was informed

that I was a social studies candidate for the Rochester City School District, but they have not yet given me a contract. He attributed this to the large bureaucracy, and the often restructuring that is associated with large urban school districts. He told the principal "that they were going to lose a strong candidate." He told the principal about me, and suggested that he takes a look at me. During our conversation, the administrator told me that this principal was expecting a call from me and I assured the administrator that I would give the principal a call. I found the entire event quite interesting; you see, not only had I not applied for a teaching position in this district, I had not even thought about applying for a position in Webster Central School District. Nevertheless, I was very anxious and excited to contact the principal. Every event has a purpose.

I called the principal, anticipating that he would be extremely busy and quite hurried; I found him to sound very warm and welcoming. He asked what day and time I could stop by his office to meet with him face-to-face. Since this was the month of August and school began the first week of September, I anticipated that I needed to stop by rather soon. I asked him, "how is tomorrow?"

As I entered Webster Schroeder Jr. High School, I noticed the cleanliness that most suburban schools possessed. The floors were shiny and buffed as if they were cleaned seconds ago; the furniture in the main office was rich as if it was made of the finest oak. The principal's secretary greeted me with a warm smile and pleasantly said "please be seated, he is expecting you and will be with you in a moment." Although, she attempted to engage in small talk, I sat there with my heart racing to the point I thought that it was going to jump out of my chest. My palms were sweaty and my mouth was so dry that I needed a mint. I swear that moment seemed as if it were an eternity. The cold reality of the situation was that I knew that I was going to get one crack at proving that I was the best candidate of more than three hundred applicants. There was a reputation, at least in my mind, that districts of this magnitude were not very open to employing professional staff of color.

The principal came to the lobby and introduced himself; his handshake was quite firm. During this handshake, I was reminded of my father's words that the firmness of a person's handshake is indicative of the level of trust that I should have for a person; the less firm, the less I should trust that person. This principal was a white male of average height in his mid to late fifties. He invited me into his office. The office was extremely spacious in terms of my comparisons and it looked as if he had spent a great deal of time working that summer. After sitting down in the chair facing his desk, the butterflies seemed to have dissipated. He was a warm gentleman with a sense of humor. He began by telling me about the eighth grade social studies teacher position. He reiterated what the administrator had told me - that there was a high volume of applications/resumes on file. For whatever reason though, I felt as if I were supposed to begin my teaching career at this school; the feeling was overwhelmingly lodged in my spirit.

Not sure if this were a formal interview or a formal discussion, the principal spoke eloquently about the Civil Rights Movement and the ugly stain that bigotry, ethnocentrism, hatred and ignorance have left on this country. I was impressed and intrigued that he was comfortable enough to discuss such a topic. He continued by talking about Medgar Evers, Dr. King, Malcolm, and a host of other people of color who have made major contributions in the lives of people in this country. I remember feeling rather astonished, wondering how his colleagues would feel and what they would think if they could hear his words at this moment. Although they might agree with him, they probably would not be bold enough to mention these things to others. This principal was well versed in his knowledge around history and we talked for several hours.

He said he saw me in the same light as the Tuskegee Airmen. If given the opportunity he felt as though I could make a major impact in the lives of the children to whom he was responsible. Little did the principal know that he had impacted my life in a major way on that hot August day.

My life at Webster Schroeder Jr. High School was quite interesting. The students were eager and somewhat curious to have me as a teacher. I know for many of them, it was their first experience having a black teacher. I depended on my faith and ability to persevere when there were incidents that reminded me that we still live in a world that is discriminatory and afraid. I was taught to believe that the human spirit permeates beyond race and ethnicity.

It was important to me that I maintain a very positive rapport with my students. I enjoyed teaching the students daily, and vividly remember one incident that has remained. There was a student whose parents had instructed her to take copious notes of my behavior and actions in the classroom. I discovered this fact when observing her nervous and fidgety behavior for about a week. I became very concerned about her noticeable discomfort. Understandably, I asked her what was troubling her and why was she always taking notes even during the times when note-taking was unnecessary. I was surprised, and bothered, to find that her parents ordered her to take notes on my interactions and every move within the classroom. It was an unfortunate situation because this student's parents could not fathom that a young, 23 year old black male was teaching their daughter. I arranged to meet the student's parents and the school administrator. During this meeting, the parents openly admitted to having issues about my ethnicity. I sat in silence as I did not find it necessary to be responsive. I was hurt and angry. However, I did feel bad for my student in that the parents' actions were teaching her bigotry. The student really enjoyed my class and I enjoyed having her in my class.   All I wanted to do was teach. I vowed not to get caught up in other people's race issues and to forgive but not forget. The school year continued and ended, and this was the first and last time that I encountered racism while teaching in the Webster Central School District.

Ethnocentrism and discrimination unfortunately can, and will, vehemently affect the human psyche. This unfortunate event reminded me of a horrible experience I had when I was five years old. As a child, I had an unshakable affinity for my father. He stood strong and tall and as far as I knew, he could move mountains. One Friday night when my father and I were alone at home, I remember being awakened at approximately 12:30 a.m., by a loud and aggressive knock at our front door. My father yelled down the hall and stairs "who is it?" I could hear the concern in my father's voice as this was not a typical occurrence. A deep masculine voice replied, "The police!" My father walked to the door, extremely cautious. In this country it is well validated as to why African American men mistrust police officers. My father had reason to proceed with caution. I remember standing at the top of the staircase as my father opened the door. Immediately, he was brutally attacked and hand-cuffed by several police officers. My father purposely did not fight back. My father repeatedly yelled my "five year old son is here!" I began to cry out profusely for my father as he was driven away on that warm summer night. I was left home alone until my mother came home from work the next morning.

Still in tears, my mother frantically asked, "what is wrong and where is your father?" As she held me in her arms, I told her that the police had handcuffed him and taken him away. She immediately called the police station and, from my mother's expression, she knew that something was not right. My father is a man of peace, highly principled and driven by integrity. My mother, siblings and I discovered he had been falsely identified and wrongly accused of a crime he did not commit. My family and I had to endure this degradation at the behest of the police force. In later years when my father and I talked about this unfortunate event, he never mentioned the ethnicity of the officers. The same forces that prevailed in the experience with my father were the same forces that resurfaced with the "situation" with my student and her parents.

Two years past and I was preparing to enter my third year at Webster Schroeder. I was excited because for a new teacher, the third year was an indication that you could be granted tenure if you demonstrated that you were competent and effective. My past evaluations reflected my competence and effectiveness; I was confident that I would become tenured. Little did I know that the universe had other plans for me.

One evening while finding my seat at the Auditorium Theatre in Rochester, New York, I noticed that my seat was in front of a woman I had not seen in several years. I immediately acknowledged her, as her sons and I used to play together before her family moved to the suburbs. We both agreed to connect in the main corridor of the theater at the end of the play. I remember thinking, what is the probability of sitting in the theater in front of someone from the "old days in the neighborhood". Every event has a purpose.

After the play, we met in the main corridor. She gave me a play-by-play update of her two sons. She then asked about my parents and my family as a whole. She finally asked me typical questions, "Did I attend college? Where did I attend? What did I major in while I was there?" I could not wait to tell her that I was preparing for my third year as a social studies teacher. I knew that this would be special to her because she was a school administrator in one of the highest achieving school districts in the State of New York. As a youngster, I had told her how much I respected her and that one day I would become a teacher.

She congratulated me and asked if I were interested in coming to Brighton Central School District? I thought she was being comical; however, she was very serious. I told her that I loved teaching in my current district. However, I could not forget the experience I had with my student's parents; subconsciously, I knew that any decision to leave Webster was influenced by this one unfortunate and unforgettable experience. She asked me for several recommendations and told me that she would pass the information on to the personnel director, principal and the superintendent. We hugged and said our good-byes. I stood there in a daze, fantasizing about what it would be like to teach in Brighton Central District, a school district with a national reputation of being "outstanding."

Several weeks passed and still no word from anyone from Brighton Central School District. Time was of the essence, and the summer was winding down and the new school year would begin soon. Although I was anxious to hear from the District, I did not have high expectations. I felt as though the likelihood of Brighton recruiting me was rather slim. I thought of contacting my former neighbor, but I disciplined myself not to do so.

Several more days past, and I came to the conclusion that I would be entering my third year of teaching in Webster Central School District. I did have a flicker of hope, however, that Brighton Central District would call. I had convinced myself that the reason no one from the District had called up to this point was that the decision makers were vacationing.

My desire to teach in the Brighton system had nothing to do with my lack of satisfaction with Webster, but Brighton, again, is one of the best school districts in the nation, and perceived by many to be the crème de la crème of school districts. To my surprise, I received the phone call from Brighton several weeks prior to the start of the new school year! I was asked to meet with the superintendent and middle school principal to discuss the possibility of teaching in the Brighton School District. This was a major opportunity!

Although I was prepared to start the school year at Webster Central School District, I also had planned to begin a Ph.D at The University of Pennsylvania; I had applied, and the likelihood of being accepted was very favorable. Nevertheless, the possibility of teaching in Brighton at this time was more attractive to me.

I found the initial meeting with the Brighton administrators quite interesting. The superintendent was a well polished individual with an air of confidence that was very assuring. Although the principal was somewhat quiet during the meeting, I could tell from his persona that he was self-assured, competent with his skills, and knew his craft well.

The superintendent indicated that an extensive background check on me had been completed. I was shocked, but impressed. The principal pointed out that the background check was important, because they did not want to waste anyone's time. He also said "it is vital that we put the brightest and best before our children. We have high expectations of excellence for our school district." After that statement was made, not only did I want to be there, I knew that I needed to be there. It was amazing how forward thinking and assertive Brighton had been in their thrust to recruit me. There was truly a power much higher than I operating.

The principal suggested that we go on a tour of the district. While admiring different aspects of a classroom, I noticed that the principal had an American History textbook in his hand; he motioned me over to where he and the superintendent were standing near a large window. To my surprise, the principal dropped the textbook out of the window! I immediately thought this was some kind of initiation and they expected me to retrieve the book from two stories below. I was prepared to tell them that I would not participate in any games of this nature, until the principal interrupted me to say "we expect you to make a major distinction between the whole story and half of the story." I asked him to clarify his comment. He talked to me about the importance of clearing up lies and misconceptions that often take place when we teach and learn about American history. The principal's conversation was somewhat similar to that of the principal from Webster Schroeder Jr. High School, but much more in-depth. Again, I found this very interesting.

Soon after our meeting, I began teaching in the Brighton Central School District. I was honored to have the flexibility to design lesson plans that were in-depth; plans that not only captured the attention of my students but told the entire history of this great country. Lesson plans that remained within the framework of the District's curriculum but afforded students the opportunity to look at the map of human existence and see the contributions of all ethnic groups. I met the principal's challenge of "the story and a half," and when I left as the Social Studies teacher in the Brighton Central School District, I knew that I had, in the words of one of America's most prolific writers, James Baldwin, raised an awareness in my students that "American history is longer, larger, more various, more beautiful, and more terrible than anyone has ever said about it."

The first day of school was interesting. Although I felt welcomed, I noticed there were students and staff alike who were not used to having a young African American male teacher. After the experiences at Webster Schroeder, I believed I had the right and the ability to teach any place in the world. After the initial introductions, the reality that the summer vacation had ended, everyone and everything settled and teaching and learning began.

Teaching in the Brighton Central School District was just another ordered step granted to me from the Creator. The beauty of Brighton is that it was diverse and open to all aspects of gaining knowledge. Although many people aggrandized Brighton as if it were larger than life, I knew that God had given me this opportunity to touch the essence of the spirit of children given to me. Every event has a purpose.

Although I only taught for five years, it was probably the most rewarding time I have experienced in the field of education. It allowed me to have direct daily contact with the world's greatest natural resource, our children. I will be forever grateful to the principals and superintendents who believed in my abilities and gave me the opportunity to teach in the districts and schools in which they led.

Chapter Three

Exposure
to Excellence

---

*"Mind Power – There is a way to provide against the onslaught of poverty.
It is the recognition of the power of the mind."*
-A. G. Gaston

Exposure to excellence has truly been a blessing to me; humans normally do what they see. There is great value and importance of maintaining positive environments that nurture and develop us into what we desire out of life. We often are products of our environments.

During my youth, I was profoundly affected by the phrase, "a mind is a terrible thing to waste." This phrase was coined by the United Negro College Fund in its efforts to increase opportunities for students of color to attend historically black colleges and universities. I vowed that I would not waste my mind or my time on things that were not positive or conducive to me living a meaning-ful life. I wanted more than just graduating from college and work-ing a job. I wanted to make a lasting impact in the lives of others and lead a life that was more aligned with a purpose. My purpose became teaching/education; not as a vocation, but devotion for years to come; simply put, education is my life's work.

I realized early that devotion alone does not educate; there must be an attitude of excellence and an altitude of the stars. Brighton Central School District had both.

I heard prior to coming to Brighton that the students were fo-cused, but I did not realize until I was actually there how high the expec-tations actually were. I must say I loved every second of the high level of discussion in which my students and I were able to engage.

I had students who were highly charged and who embraced the importance of a quality education. They were centered and focused on instruction, but at the same time it was quite evident that many of the students had world experiences outside of the classroom. In fact, many of the children had already traveled abroad and been exposed to other cultures. These students were able to provide a wealth of personal life stories to various discus-sions and lessons. They were talented, some gifted and certainly in tune with high expectations, both intrinsically and extrinsically. My experience was awesome; however, I would not forget what happened one day late in the month of June. Two students, one of them I had in my class and the other I knew from coaching football were killed.

I remember getting out of bed on a Saturday, and turning on the talk radio station that I listened to every morning. Regular programming was interrupted for a special report. The report was about two children who were hit by a train the evening before. To my surprise, I found out that they were the two students of whom I had become very fond. According to accounts, they died on impact. I was shocked to hear of this tragedy and to find out that they were my students. I could not understand why and how something like this could happen. After calling and talking to several colleagues, I found out that the students were with other children. The group of children was walking and decided to take a short cut. Unfortunately, the short cut included crossing a railroad track. All of the students except one made it across; the one student's foot was stuck in the track. She began to panic as the train moved forward at a rapid pace. The other student attempted a heroic rescue on her behalf. Unfortunately, the oncoming train could not brake and fatally struck both students. The families, school district, and the Brighton community had suffered a major loss by losing these two special young people. When children die, there is a sense of questioning why. I remember the loss of my young nephew Jerrod. He and his friend found a gun; they thought the gun was empty, but one bullet was lodged in the chamber. The friend pulled the trigger and the bullet struck Jerrod in his aorta; he fell back into a chair and exclaimed to his friend, "Don't worry about it." He died immediately thereafter. My nephew was only seventeen and a great kid. What a terrible loss to this universe for these three great kids and the many others I have known who have died tragically before their time. There is no way to explain an event that results in the death of a child. These events impacted my life in a major way.

As a product of urban public education, I always envisioned myself teaching in that environment; yet I found myself struggling with my commitment to urban education in that after five years I still had not taught in an urban district. As I mentioned earlier, I had applied to the urban district from which I had graduated but was not hired because of laden bureaucracy.

Many of my African American colleagues frequently questioned me about why I was teaching in Brighton. Sometimes I responded by asking "do you question the high number of white teachers who teach in predominantly African American school districts?" Usually, there was no response, just silence. Some people are comfortable in certain school districts; I felt that I was competent and I cared enough for all children to teach successfully in any place. All children have the potential to become high achievers and masters of excellence. It is the responsibility of the educator to ensure that this happens.

One day late in the evening in the month of April, the feeling of spring was beginning to sit in; I walked over to the Superintendent's office, hoping he was still there. Although I had strong aspirations of becoming an administrator and eventually a school superintendent, I had not had the discussion with the District's superintendent. I went to his office for two reasons: I felt like I needed clarity and guidance from him; and secondly, I needed to know if there were future opportunities for a leadership position within the Brighton system. Fortunately, for me, he was in his office. I shared with him my strong desire of one day becoming a school superintendent; he punned by saying that I could have his job. Unfortunately, this was not a laughing matter to me. He shared his thoughts about me becoming an administrator; however, when I talked about future opportunities in the Brighton system, he was cautiously optimistic. Although he was somewhat reserved, he told me "I believe that you will make a good administrator in our district." He advised me to secure my administrative degree and obtain a doctorate. He insisted that I apply to the University of Rochester, which is where he received his Doctorate. He boasted about the outstanding experience he had there. Although I enjoyed teaching history and coaching varsity football and basketball, my overwhelming passion for leadership and the haunting thought of urban education still loomed.

About a week later I shared the conversation that I had with the superintendent with the school principal. He was rather pleased and encouraged me to give leadership further thought. I knew the principal was retiring in the next year or two and he was thinking about his successor. The principal agreed that I should apply for the administrative program at the University of Rochester and then obtain my doctorate. He reminded me that the school district not only would pay my tuition but pay for the cost of my books etc.; this was a deal I knew I could not refuse.

Chapter Four

The Doctorate

"One's work may finish one day, but one's education shall never end."
-Alexander Dumas

I applied to the University of Rochester's program and was accepted. When I met with the chair of the Education Department, he seemed, like so many others, to have a great deal of respect for the Brighton Central School District. A staunch conservative, he and I shared similar views. He also mentioned that the District's superintendent had called him about me and was very complimentary. I did not comment initially, but as he praised Brighton even more by saying it is well represented by excellent leadership and high competent faculty and staff, I finally acknowledged his sentiments by stating "I am honored to be a part of a district that is recognized nationally for student achievement." At this point I think we both realized it was imperative to transition the conversation.

The Education Department chair volunteered information he felt was important. He informed me that the percentage of African American students was very small and of that population the majority was females. Although I knew he felt rather obligated to tell me this, I do not think his intent was derogatory. He spoke honestly about the reality of what existed within the University of Rochester as a whole and the Margaret Warner School of Education in particular. He was very concerned with students having the ability to handle the academic rigor that necessitated success at the University. From this point on, I knew that he and I would become friends.

I did well academically, and completed the necessary course work to receive my building administrator and central administration (superintendent's) certification/license. However, I found many of my courses to be couched in a great deal of theory. It is my belief that one should be competent in their area of expertise along with possessing general knowledge that all educators should have around pedagogy, methods and best practices.

I had taken several courses with the Education Department chair and was impressed with his knowledge of educational law and quantitative and qualitative research. This is where my love of research began. I would visit his office to have additional discussions of educational law, politics and the contemporary state of education. He introduced me to the concept of democracy within education. The conversations would take us down paths of Plessey vs. Ferguson, Brown vs. The School Board of Topeka Kansas, to the infancy stages of the No Child Left Behind legislation. He encouraged me to apply and continue on to complete my doctorate degree. I was accepted into the Doctoral program, successfully completed some courses but transferred to the University of Buffalo. I transferred from the University of Rochester, because I left Brighton Central for a principalship in the Rochester City School District School. I wanted to confer a doctorate at U of R, but it would have been difficult for me to continue to pay out of pocket in that the Rochester City School District made it clear that you have to be an employee at least three years before they reimburse for doctoral courses. I completed the doctoral program at the University of Buffalo. Without a doubt, there is validity in having a doctorate. Going through the process allowed me to understand the value of knowing how to provide independent research and apply it to day-to-day operations.

Chapter Five

The Gap

"The reality of urban education and the plight of many African American children is that many of these children are being left behind, even with the No Child Left Behind legislation. Education, and not entertainment or sports, must be embraced as a realistic escape from generational poverty."

-Me

One evening while jogging through my neighborhood, I encountered the newly appointed Superintendent of the Rochester City School District. I interrupted my run to introduce myself. He and I conversed for around twenty minutes; it is amazing how much you can find out about a person in a short conversation! I shared with him my desire to become a school administrator and then a school Superintendent. I told him that I was a teacher in Brighton schools; he seemed rather impressed that I taught in Brighton. I also mentioned that I was in the final stages of obtaining my administrative certification at the University of Rochester. I added that in order for me to complete the graduation requirements, I had to do an internship. I shared with him my desire to be in urban education. This newly appointed superintendent encouraged me to do my internship during the upcoming summer in the Rochester City School District. He gave me several names to contact. I did as he instructed and was able to secure an internship that summer at Frederick Douglass Middle School as an administrator. Every event has a purpose.

I had a great experience that summer. I was convinced that I was an asset for many of the students and staff with whom I came into contact. As the summer was winding down I was contemplating my next strategy. I knew that I would have completed my certification requirements and would be prepared to possibly return to Brighton as an administrator. As fate would have it, that never happened. While wrapping up my last week at Frederick Douglass, I was summoned to the main office. I had received a call from the Human Resources Department at Central Administration. I was informed that the Superintendent wanted to offer me an administrative contract. I was asked if I could meet with the Human Resources Office the next day; of course, I excitedly complied. When I arrived the next day at the Human Resources Office, I was very surprised to see that the newly appointed Director of Human Resources was one of the teachers who sparked my desire to become an educator! Talk about coming full circle! Destiny arrived at my doorstep. Finally, I was going to embark upon the chance to serve as an administrator in the district that I initially set out to teach. Dreams do come true.

I informed Human Resources that I had to resign from Brighton Central Schools and I did just that. I knew that I would not be able to teach or coach football the upcoming season; however, I had to move on. I personally submitted my letter of resignation to the superintendent and the principal. I was shocked to find out that they already knew. The superintendent said that the Superintendent of Rochester City School District had spoken to him several weeks prior, demonstrating great interest in hiring me in a leadership role in RCSD. He said the superintendent of RCSD and a host of others were impressed with me. I asked for their blessings as I cleaned my classroom and said my goodbyes that warm summer day.

My administrative position with the RCSD was at a middle school. I had an incredible experience, and after one year was promoted and became director of an alternative program that included thirteen independent sites. I was considered to be on a fast track and earned several other promotions. My time spent in the Rochester City School District was rich: I had several principalships and positions within Central Administration. I was considered an agent of reform.

As an agent of reform, I witnessed the cold reality of African American students struggling in the urban public schools of Rochester. For many of these children education was a matter of life or death. Research supports that education and the security of the nation are interlocked in that there is a direct correlation between one's educational level and the propensity to commit a crime.

The literature on education and social science is replete with articles, books, and other sources relative to the woeful state of poor and urban communities, particularly aspects of the African American community. While few would argue that America's contemporary urban educational structure (kindergarten through twelfth grade) is perfect, this structure remains the norm in most urban school districts. Today, many urban public school districts across America, if not all, continue to demonstrate a commitment similar to principles followed by earlier educational institutions. Many will contend that poor, urban children are under siege, and are viewed from a distance as invisible children.

Unfortunately, history proves the experience for African Americans' quest for educational equality was entirely different from other ethnicities. The "founding fathers" had no intentions of educating African Americans. Therefore, the more recent historical impact on learning environments today is important to note because after the Civil War, segregated educational facilities were maintained under the policy of separate but equal. After more than fifty years since Brown vs. The Board of Education, the struggle to provide a quality education for every child regardless of ethnicity continues. I am passionate about educating all children.

We cannot ignore the achievement gap! The dynamics of today's urban school environments have become more complex and diverse. In a rapidly changing and increasingly technologically oriented society, students need to acquire the knowledge and skills that will help them achieve success in school and in life. Education was for me, and still is for many other children, a matter of life or death.

Chapter Six

Everyone Needs A Mentor

"It must be borne in the mind that the tragedy of life does not lie in not reaching your goals, the tragedy lies in not having any goals to reach. It isn't a calamity to die with dreams unfulfilled, but is a calamity not to dream. It is not a disaster to be unable to capture your ideas, but it is a disaster to have no ideas to capture. It is not a disgrace not to reach the stars, but it is a disgrace not to have any stars to reach."
-Benjamin Mays

There are many lessons that I have learned about forming valuable relationships from my father, mentors and a host of others along the way. I have discovered the following: we can not go at it alone; you have to value your support team and no matter what happens, love always wins.

My course work in Leadership and Policy at the University of Buffalo included a Superintendent's internship. I instantly thought of the superintendent of Rochester City Schools; however, he had already committed to work with another intern from Harvard and felt that "it would be rather challenging to commit to two interns at once."

I understood, but the reality was that I had to find a Superintendent somewhere in the country that would sponsor me. I called upon my mentor. I advise any aspiring Superintendent to find a mentor, preferably another superintendent. My mentor was the Superintendent of Mount Clemens School District in Mount Clemens, Michigan, and had served as Superintendent in various places across the country. He eagerly said yes. My mentor explained the benefits of not doing the internship in my home district. I requested and received permission from the University of Buffalo to complete my internship out-of-state. I drove to Mount Clemens, Michigan for almost a year to spend three days a month working with my mentor.

My internship with my mentor was an excellent introduction to the ascension of becoming a Superintendent. He is an awesome educator. He methodically introduced me to concepts and situations that would be relevant to a superintendent. While the superintendent may delegate duties and responsibilities, he/she maintains final authority and accountability. This internship taught me that while on the surface, being a Superintendent is a high profile job, it is definitely not one of glamour. Necessary attributes of successful school superintendents include but are not limited to tenacity, courage, leadership skills, self-confidence, high self esteem, intelligence, passion, effective communication, both verbally and in the written format, and most importantly, the ability to love children.

The role of a School Superintendent is very demanding; the charge is very challenging, and it definitely is not a position for those who are faint at heart. I feel that it is imperative that that I share with you the roles and responsibilities of a School Superintendent.

They are as follows:

Relationship with the School Board

1. Serve as the executive officer for the Board of Education and be charged with the responsibility of implementing the policies of the School Board. He/she shall attend and participate in all regular, special and executive meetings of the Board except portions of executive sessions held to discuss the Superintendent's contract or performance;

2. Develop a harmonious working relationship with the School Board. He/She shall treat all School Board members impartially. He/She shall go to the Board when serious differences of opinion arise in a earnest effort to resolve such differences immediately;

3. Serve as a resource person and advisor to the School Board. He/She shall keep the School Board informed on issues, needs,

and operation of the school system. He/She shall advise the School Board, based on thorough study and analysis, on items requiring Board action;

4. Provide appraisal of all school policies originating with the School Board. He/she shall advise the School Board on the need for new and/or revised policies and suggest draft policies to satisfy those needs;

5. Coordinate preparation of each Board meeting's agenda with Board President;

Education Direction and Leadership

6. Enforce all provisions of law, rules and regulations, and Board policy relating to the management of the schools and other educational, social and recreational activities. He/She shall develop administrative procedures to implement Board policy. He/She shall be available to interpret for the staff all Board policies and applicable laws, rules and regulations;

7. Supervise, understand and keep informed on all aspects of the instructional program. He/She review and update the educational program of the school district and keep the School Board informed of all changes in curriculum;

8. Encourage a positive approach to student behavior and discipline, enforce the compulsory attendance law and supervise the performance of the school attendance officer(s);

9. Recommend to the School Board for its adoption all courses of study, curriculum guides and textbooks to be used in the schools;

10. Direct the preparation of the Comprehensive Assessment Report;

Personnel

11. Evaluate annually the performance of each administrator who directly reports to the Superintendent;

12. Coordinate with the administrative staff the evaluation of all instructional personnel, the development of job descriptions for new instructional positions, and the periodic review of existing job descriptions for instructional personnel;

13. Recommend personnel action to the School Board (e.g., appointments, assignments, leaves of absences, suspensions, terminations);

14. Coordinate development of district staffing needs;

15. Encourage participation of appropriate staff members in long range planning;

16. Communicate achievements and, when appropriate, concerns of personnel to the School Board;

17. Coordinate the updating of the district directory, staff manuals and handbooks for procedures;

Financial Management

18. Work closely with the administrative staff in the management and operation of the fiscal affairs of the school district;

19. Prepare and present to the Board a preliminary annual budget in accordance with a schedule established with the Board. He/She is responsible for ensuring that the budget, as adopted by the School Board and approved at the annual meeting, is properly administered. He/She shall ensure that regular reports are made to the School Board on the status of the Budget;

20. Establish efficient procedures to maximize income; safeguard investments and provide effective controls for all expenditures of school funds in accordance with adopted budget. He/She shall ensure that all necessary bookkeeping and accounting records are maintained by the district.

Contract Negotiations, Administration and Interpretation

21. Monitor negotiated contracts to assure that contractual obligations are fairly administered;

22. Review recommendations for changes in policies, regulations and procedures resulting from negotiations;

23. Receive and process contractual and non-contractual grievances;
24. Review completed contracts with appropriate personnel;

Community Relations

25. Establish and maintain open communications with the community;

26. Seek the respect and support of the community in the conduct of school district operations. He/She shall keep the public informed about the policies, practices and problems in the district's schools, and provide leadership in changing attitudes and practices for the future;

27. Solicit and consider opinions and concerns of groups and individuals;

28. Work effectively with the public and private sector. Establish and maintain an effective working relationship with all segments of the community: parent-teacher organizations, local and state government, other school systems, institutions, agencies, civic organizations, and the general public;

29. Coordinate district public relations information (newspaper, calendar, etc.). He/She shall develop friendly and cooperative relationships with the news media;

Facilities Management

30. Oversee the supervision of operations, maintenance, alterations and repair to building and grounds, insisting on competent and efficient performance;

31. Evaluate facility needs and recommend to the Board improvement, alterations and changes in the buildings, grounds, and equipment of the district;

Professional Performance

32. Defend principles and convictions in the face of pressure and partisan influence;

33. Earn respect and standing among professional colleagues;

34. Devote time and energy effectively to the duties of Superintendent;

35. Exercise judgment in making decisions;

Management Functions

36. Coordinate and manage the district so the school organization operates smoothly and efficiently. He/She shall strive to coordinate the planning, organizational, decision-making, problem solving, and communication processes to achieve effectiveness in all areas of the school district;

37. Perform such other duties as the majority of the School Board may determine and/or as established by the Superintendents Contract;

38. Determine whether schools should close due to emergencies

(inclement weather, road conditions, building conditions, etc.) and make appropriate provisions for emergency management planning;

Personal Qualities and Growth

39. To demonstrate outstanding qualities of leadership with ability to delegate authority and responsibility effectively and to hold subordinates accountable;

40. To speak well before large and small groups, expressing ideas in a logical and forthright manner;

41. To maintain professional development by reading and course work, attending conferences, working on professional committees, visiting other districts, and meeting with other Superintendents.

My most valued mentor did a magnificent job exposing me to the aforementioned items. He spent a great deal of time not only modeling strong positive relationships with students, school board, community, bargaining units, parents, businesses, agencies, etc., he also consistently stressed the significance of those relationships.

Towards the final stages of my internship, I was invited to lunch by my mentor to discuss the final project and talk about the evaluative process of my performance. As we drove to the restaurant, we were engaged in small talk; I was becoming quite anxious to get to the heart of the matter, the evaluation! After we were seated in the restaurant and the waitress took our order, he began by telling me that I did an excellent job on my final project. For the final project, my mentor and the School Board had requested a comparative analysis on a nation wide educational management company that partnered with districts to provide a different landscape that could potentially raise student achievement versus the traditional schools' approach to raising student achievement. The study indicated that this particular management company showed no significant gains, actually it had become quite a drain on the budget for the school district.

As we transitioned into the next topic at hand, which seemed to purposely be delayed, he talked about other insignificant issues. I was overcome by a strong surge of curiosity. Then, he finally made the leap. He said that he was going to give me an excellent evaluation and admired my commitment to completing the internship. He said that I exemplified the qualities of effective leadership and was not afraid of challenges or obstacles. His next statement, however, blew me away; he said that I should start thinking about becoming a superintendent! I was stunned; this was a powerful statement coming from someone whom I consider an excellent superintendent. Although becoming a school superintendent was my ultimate goal, I did not see myself realistically accomplishing this until I was at least in my forties. My mentor said that I should set a goal for myself to become a superintendent by the age of thirty six because it was clear to him that I had all of the skills, and he wanted to make sure that as an African American male I did not "sell myself short." From that day on, he groomed me and spent countless hours advising me.

The internship ended, and the superintendent of Rochester City School District continued to take notice in my work-ethic and drive. During the next several years, he provided several opportunities in leadership at the building level and in central administration. It was rumored that I was being groomed to become Superintendent of RCSD. I continued to talk with my wife, Lisa, about my goal of becoming a Superintendent. My wife has been my main support; she has believed in me at times when I have had difficulty believing in myself. Her love, courage and commitment have been the cohesion that has kept our family moving in the right direction. She is not only my wife, she is also my friend. She speaks with wisdom and maturity; I admire her to the highest degree. She, like my mentor, believed that I could not only take on the position of School Superintendent, but become a successful superintendent. She has consistently spoken of my passion for education and my love for children: she understands the struggles of an African American male striving to become the top educator of a school district.

Lisa began to encourage me to apply for various superintendent vacancies. She would do the necessary research on the school districts and share the information with me. I began traveling to various parts of the country meeting people and applying for positions. I had been rejected on numerous occasions; some districts did not even bother to respond. I felt dejected and rejected. I was self absorbed in my defeat and became content in my current role. My wife refused to participate in my pity party! She continued to encourage me to stay focused on my goal. She was, and still is, my constant support. One day she told me about the position with the Fallsburg Central School District located near New York City. She said that I should at least go through the application process. I looked at the brochure and did not see a single African American student. From past racial experiences, I immediately felt that getting an interview with this District would be a challenge. Boy, was I wrong; you really can't judge a school district by its brochure! My wife told me that if I were granted the opportunity to interview, I would land the position. Her statement not only resonated in my spirit, but proved to be true. Guys, we need to remember that our wives are blessings and are given a sixth sense by God to sometimes see things that our bravado does not allow us to.

Chapter Seven

My Fallsburg Experience

"Whatever you can do, or dream you can, begin it.
Boldness has genius, power and magic in it."
-W.H. Murray

I followed Lisa's advice and applied for the position of Superintendent of Schools for the Fallsburg Central School District. I telephoned the person responsible for conducting the search and introduced myself. He was cordial, quite professional and chose his words carefully. I told him that I was currently a principal in the Rochester City School District and shared some of my background and experiences. He told me about the district and the community (Fallsburg). I listened intently and requested a face-to-face meeting. In a calm demeanor, he told me that at this "juncture he and the Board were just screening paperwork submitted by the forty or more candidates." I thought to myself, wow, forty or more candidates. He ended our telephone conversation with "nice speaking with you and good luck." I had vowed to Lisa, and myself, that I would not get discouraged; I immediately began to pray. I prayed for the spirit of strength and the ability to move through the process without getting overly anxious. Prayer has and always will be the source of my strength.

Several days had passed and I found myself in a state of unusual peace. I was determined not to overanalyze the situation, so I focused on my students, parents, faculty and staff. Then out of no where I received a call from my wife, Lisa, informing me that the man responsible for the search had called requesting that he meets with me to conduct a screening on behalf of the School Board. He asked that I contact him to schedule a date and time. The next day I excitedly returned the call and confirmed a date and time for us to get together. I knew that I had to do my homework for this meeting and spent the next week and a half doing extensive research on the school district, community and the county.

Sullivan County as a whole, Fallsburg in particular, had a long rich legacy of Jewish influence. Many Jewish people either migrated from New York City to live in the area year round or had summer homes. Many of them came from wealthy and influential backgrounds. Many minority citizens migrated from the South and New York City to work in the hotels in that tourism was the primary industry at that time. In recent years, the two major employers have become the correctional facilities and the school district. There was a great deal of old wealth in the community. The community was quite unique in that it had a very small middle class;

it was primarily the wealthy and the working poor. During the mid twentieth century, the hotel industry was viable and booming. Within the last 35 years or so, the area has dwindled, a lot of the wealth accumulated from the hotel and tourist industry has evaporated. Unfortunately, as a result of the declining economic base, various aspects of the community looked deserted. After my research on the area, I called a good friend, a retired Superintendent, to get some background about the district.

My friend proved to be well versed in information regarding Fallsburg. He said that there are "various aspects of the community that appear deserted, and many people thought that casinos were coming to revitalize the county through revenue." He also said "the position was a great opportunity, but it would be a tough sale to move there permanently; he was quite emphatic."

I arrived at the District Superintendent's office of the Sullivan County Board Of Cooperative Extension Services (BOCES). District Superintendents in New York State are appointed by the Commissioner of Education and report directly to the Commissioner. As I waited in the lobby area, I silently recited one of my most sacred quotes about leadership: "One significant test of quality leadership is how well the leader copes with disappointments, defeats, or some overriding adversity." Voltaire, in praising the Duke of Marlborough, called it, "calm courage in the midst of tumult;" that serenity of soul in danger, which is the greatest gift of nature for command. Finally, I was invited into the District Superintendent's office. It was extremely spacious and full of law periodicals and a library that included material centered on leadership and organizational theory.

The District Superintendent was quite expressive. His language was colorful; he used a lot of colloquialisms as he talked about himself and his experiences. I find that this is a behavior employed by many, especially males, as if we have to convince ourselves as to who we are and what we have accomplished. I spent about ninety minutes in this meeting; mostly listening to him. His candor was refreshing and I appreciated his honesty. He said to me "New York State has approximate seven hundred and twenty five school districts, only about twenty one of them are led by African Americans, and this concerns me." I asked him about the community's sentiment around ethnicity. He clearly expressed that the community was open to having someone of my caliber and ethnicity lead the district. I knew that this man was a good person.

During the application process, I felt that the probability of me landing the superintendent position was slim to impossible but I stood on God's word: faith, the substance of things hoped for, the evidence of things not seen (Hebrews 11:1). All of my predecessors had been white males, with an exception of one white female, and all were middle-aged. My perception was that they were oblivious to the ethnic and economic divide of the community, or so privileged that the divide was not a necessary focal point.

There were 39 candidates who initially applied for the position; several decided not to continue the process. The process was quite competitive to say the least. Through screening and interviewing the search pool was narrowed to six semifinalists. I was one of those individuals, and at that point, it became a reality that I had a possible chance of being selected as Superintendent. After the round of interviews were over, I was notified that I was a finalist; this alone caused reason for me to celebrate.

My last interview was inclusive of the community, and that is when I became aware of some of the ethnic and class differentiation. I told myself the first thing that I wanted to find out was if there were a clear understanding of how schools felt about parents and families and how parents and families felt about the school district. After a challenging selection process, I was appointed as the superintendent. The other finalist was a 19-year veteran superintendent in the state of New Jersey. This was my first superintendency and I was excited. Every event has a purpose.

Fallsburg is a small rural school district of approximately 1,350 students with one elementary school, one middle school, and one high school. The student population is comprised of 40% minority (18% African American and 19.5% Latino) and 7.2% English language learners.

Although many whites and the vast majority of Jewish people felt that Fallsburg was a diverse, loving and welcoming melting pot, I begged to differ. I found the area not only racially polarized, but it was also extremely class conscious. The majority of the Black and Hispanic citizens were in the lower economic strata. There was a preservation of culture on both ends. The racial tension was always subtle and hidden but at the same time it had the potential to erupt at any moment.

Clearly, in this rural area I broke the mold. I was an anomaly- a thirty-something African American male hired as the first minority superintendent in the district!

I began my tenure in July, knowing that I had to acclimate myself with policy and procedures prior to the first day of school. However, I realized that my success was contingent on the relationship that I established with the community. Therefore, I committed myself to making home visits for the first three months, introducing myself to a host of parents, students and other community stakeholders. Not only did I visit residents, I made certain that I visited places of worship, synagogues, churches, recreational facilities, town hall meetings and community gatherings. In addition, I had a host of town-hall meetings. I provided workshops for parents and staff, superintendent's round tables with parents and students which served as excellent ways in which to build bridges. I knew that I had to be more than the top educator; I had to connect with everyone in the community; after all, education is or should be a community affair.

Those home visits proved successful, and propelled families to gain a sense of trust and familiarity with me. Parents would often talk about their like or disdain with the school system. I found that many parents of color felt a major disconnect with the district, while others thought it had a rich tradition and provided a quality educational experience for their children.

Many African Americans within the Fallsburg community respected me and at times thought of me as their wizard with the magic wand to correct all of their educational woes. However, I wondered if my time in Fallsburg was for the short haul. As a result, I made sure to embrace them while at the same time maintain my distance. By keeping my distance, I felt that I was protecting both of us from pain that often accompanies separation and departure.

As an African American, I understood the Black community, but did not admire nor accept some of the community members' passivity. I encouraged them to be more vocal, sometimes to no avail. In Fallsburg, many parents within the African-American community had bad experiences within the school district, which appeared to get worse with each generation of African American children. Many of the faculty and staff believed that issues around ethnicity did not exist. I found this rather disturbing because it was almost perceived as if the children and families of color were invisible. Having any kind of discussion around this issue was not a consideration of this school district. As superintendent, this mountain was almost impossible to climb without the proper harness of support.

After more than two years of working within the district, opportunity found its way to my door. A fraternity brother, the outgoing superintendent in Syracuse, New York, encouraged me to apply for the superintendent job in Syracuse. This same fraternity brother had a good relationship with the search firm and advocated on my behalf. I was a non–traditional candidate because of my age and limited experience. My application was one of many from across the country. The application and selection processes were very stringent, and the applicant pool was very competitive. From the many applications screened, approximately thirty were selected for interviews; I was among the thirty. From the pool of thirty, I became one of two finalists. My emotions ran very high and I felt that even if I were not selected as the superintendent, this process validated that my skills equaled, if not exceeded, those of some of the country's most renowned and respected educators. The sixth sense of my wife and my faith in a higher power were truly at work. The hiring committee and the Board members struggled with choosing between us, and required an additional two weeks to make a final decision. In the end, I was not chosen. Every event has a purpose.

The search firm working with the Syracuse District was also conducting a search for the East St. Louis and Flint School Districts. The search firm recruited me for both districts. In the meantime, however, the applicant chosen for Syracuse resigned after several days on the job. Syracuse then asked if I were still interested in the possibility of serving as superintendent. When this call came from Syracuse, however, I had accepted an offer from Flint Community Schools and was in the process of contract negotiations. Although I would have liked to have received an offer from Syracuse, at this juncture it would have been disingenuous to renege on my acceptance to Flint.

Unfortunately, the story of my intent to leave Fallsburg hit the press before I had an opportunity to speak with any of the Fallsburg Board members. My Board president and other members contacted me during my family vacation and tried to dissuade me from leaving Fallsburg. There was a genuine concern for my professional well being if I went to Flint because of Flint's eroding economy and the long-standing problems that had plagued the school district. More importantly, Fallsburg was very pleased with my performance and the increase in student achievement. There have been moments in which I pondered what would have happened had I taken the advice of those concerned members of the Fallsburg community. The Fallsburg Central School District and the many others who make up the community will always be special to me. My superintendent's journey began there, and for that start I will forever be grateful. Every event has a purpose.

Chapter Eight

Flint Community Schools:

"My District Reform Became My Storm"

"Mr. Controversy; he should have known; he lied on his resume; he is an outsider, he is from New York; he is all style and no substance; he is a reformer; he believes in top down management; he made changes for the sake of changes; he does not know our community; he is a city slickster; he is Mr. Excitement!"

I guarantee that every person is in one of three categories in life: They are headed into a storm, they are in the midst of a storm or they are just coming out of a storm. Storms come to shake us up and see what we are made of; they serve a purpose. If I can offer anything, I would say, please stay the course. There is worth in enduring the storm and never giving up. Without storms we will not appreciate the fair – weather days.

Hard to believe, right? Trust me, all of this and more were said by my dissenters; this was just the beginning of the Storm!

I left Fallsburg to become superintendent of Flint Community Schools, in Flint, Michigan. In comparison, Fallsburg had less than 2,000 students who were majority Caucasian. The faculty and staff in Fallsburg were 98.9% White. Flint had approximately 18,000 students who are predominantly African American and the faculty and staff are 70% White. I was excited and welcomed this new challenge to lead an urban school district.

When I began my educational journey, I knew that I eventually wanted to lead a large urban district. I wanted to develop reforms that would close the learning and achievement gaps as evident in the numerous research projects I had completed. Accepting the top position in Flint Community Schools was seen as the ultimate opportunity to not only expand my skill set but to favorably impact a district in dire need of reforms that would begin to narrow some of the research-based educational gaps. One day while sitting alone in my box-laden Flint office, the impact of this move hit me! I left a quaint, rural district in New York for an urban city, the birth place of General Motors Corporation. A city currently ranked as one of the most dangerous cities in the United States. In education, Michigan is ranked in the lower percentile within the nation, and the Flint School District is in the lower percentile of the school districts within the state. Little did I know when I signed the four year contract, a world was opening that was completely *foreign* to me. Needless to say, my landing was far from smooth and I was in for an even bumpier ride for the next several months!

My Flint experience was tumultuous from day one. I was met with a great deal of resistance from various groups who strongly endorsed an inside candidate who had approximately forty years of working in the district. A district with a graduation rate of thirty-seven percent; aging buildings; archaic technology; low academic expectations; high suspension and expulsion rates K–12. The community seemed disenfranchised with adult agendas that interfered with educating children. All of these were red flags; however, I had begun the relocation process from New York and felt that it was too late to reconsider. On top of all of this, the Board's treasurer vehemently fought, and won, to reduce the starting annual salary that was posted at the time of my application; I was grossly underpaid for the challenges that faced me.

There was a large portion of the community who saw me as a beacon of hope and that I would serve as some liberating force for the children of Flint. Hope for the future, but there was a cancerous force that attempted to stamp out hope. Flint is a community that has suffered a great deal of loss. One of the Board members referred to Flint as the family that had a great deal of wealth until one day they lost everything and were unable to recover. Many people within the community continuously reminisced about the good-old days without having the ability to ground themselves with a Plan B. Nostalgic stories and interludes of faded wishes of the return of yesteryear are pervasive throughout the community. I hope that the citizens of Flint can get beyond this state of denial.

The school system was at the brink of state takeover and I was hired to save the district. As one of the youngest Superintendents to ever lead the Flint Community Schools, I was perceived as a panacea by some and a destructionist by others. My aggressive reform plan, approved by the Board of Education members, became the noose for my high-tech lynching. Never mind that the Governor, State Superintendent and a host of others applauded the aggressive reform plan, there were those in the community who saw me as the enemy, causing a ripple effect that would shake their mere existence. At every turn, Mr. Controversy and Mr. Excitement raised their ugly heads.

Before I could begin my work in Flint there were missteps. Some created by me and others orchestrated. First, there was an issue with my credentials on the online application and resume submitted to the search firm; the information regarding a master's appeared on the wrong line, which I was not able to correct. However, I clarified it later in another section of the online application and notified the Board and the search firm of this error. Please note in order for me to have served as a Superintendent in New York State, I had to have administrative and superintendent certifications. It required rigorous academic and practical experiences to acquire certification beyond a Master's Degree. The State of Michigan only requires a Master's Degree, not a Master's Degree and a state certification. Now, here is where the politics began. A Board member and others within and outside of the Flint School System who were not in favor of my candidacy leaked this information along with their embellishments to the press, and the games began. I was accused of erroneously stating that I had two Masters and a Doctorate before I obtained my Doctorate from the University of Buffalo. From that point on and continuing for the next eighteen months, whether real or created, controversy was the storm.

The groups/forces attempted to defame, slander, and salaciously attack my character. It was more than politics; it was personal. They tried to manipulate the general public with a smear campaign that depicted me as not the right person to lead Flint Community Schools. One of the community alternative papers went so far as to characterize me as a hooded figure in black face, with large white eyes, carrying a staff and called the "Teflon Man" from Far East! Ethnocentrism at its most blatant, and not a word from the local chapter of the NAACP! I felt attacked and knew that these mean-spirited acts went beyond the scope of what any human being should have to endure to be a public servant. I lost a great deal of respect for the local media, especially the local newspapers. Many of the things written were not substantiated with facts. They seemed to be committed to "gotcha" reporting and operating from rumors and innuendos. I had always had a positive relationship with the press, and this experience shook me to my core and raised questions about the integrity of these local newspapers. I often had moments where I felt all alone. I had bouts of not trusting others, no matter how sincerely they approached me. The constant attacks had begun to take its toll on me. I continuously asked myself, "How some people so focused on their own agendas can set out to destroy a young man whose only intent was to reform a dysfunctional educational system?" I wanted to help many children who had become collateral damage in a learning environment intent on keeping them ignorant and unmarketable. I have been, and always will be, a proponent of the federal mandates which have been legislated to demand that all children are educated to the optimum. The storm had gained momentum and was spiraling into a tornado!

Secondly, at my urging, the Flint Community School Board hired as a consultant a colleague of mine with whom I had worked on educational projects in Fallsburg, New York. His past work was very impressive and I felt that his core competencies would benefit the reform process. He and I worked together for about ten months developing the Reform Plan. When the time came for deployment of the reform components, my colleague was hired, at my encouragement, as Executive Director for Curricula and Instruction, a key role to ensure that responsibilities and accountability of the reform initiatives were in place at each school. A mandated background check by the State of Michigan surfaced a 1996 sexual misconduct misdemeanor in Atlanta, Georgia, for which he had supposedly pled guilty. Some people went wild, bordering on mob mentality! I endured a five-hour, grueling Board meeting attack with over six hundred people in attendance. The State Police were called in to maintain order. Many of the people in attendance were my supporters and were confident that I did not, and would not, knowingly employ anyone who could violate another human being. Note that days before this Board meeting, I had received the background information, discussed it with him, and he told me that it was not true. However, in the best interest of the school district and the parents who entrusted their children to us, his continued employment would be a distraction. At that time, I did not have the luxury to debate his guilt or innocence and I asked him to resign or face termination; he resigned. Clearly, this Board meeting was reactionary to a situation that had already in my mind been resolved. From the experience, it became clear to me that the Flint community is oftentimes reactionary to emotions and volatile behaviors without all of the facts. They call it passion; however, the critical thinkers might consider this behavior emotional overload. My storm had spiraled into a tornado that seemed to be wreaking destruction at every turn!

The press had a field day with what "I should have known; why didn't I know; when did I know it; did I know; and, if I did know, why didn't I tell?" In the media's attempts to sensationalize this story, no one in my personal arena was safe. At every turn, a media camera occasionally was at my door filming my wife and children. Hounding my family was the most severe violation of my privacy. My colleague and I were both hounded for months, and he was literally run out of town in shame and humiliation. This supposed guilty plea was the result of a questionable signature on the plea document. Months later, through my own analysis, I concluded that the Flint law authorities may have known that there were questions and discrepancies around the accuracy of this Atlanta charge. However, they charged him with not registering as a sex offender and demanded that he return to Flint to respond to this charge. When he returned, and while already at the courthouse, he was chained, shackled and paraded around like a slave on an auction block. When the local media repeatedly showed this image of my shackled colleague, I was reminded of the extent to which dirty politics pollute communities. The realization was that if this kind of torture could be imposed on him, the same, or worse, could become my fate. It became obvious to me that the intention was to find him guilty of any charge and somehow charge me with harboring a convicted felon! The powers-to-be had a plan that many felt was fueled by ethnocentrism. According to many reports, Michigan is one of the most segregated states in the United States and Flint is one of the most segregated cities in Michigan. My experiences often made me wonder if the fire exhibited by the Flint black community during the late sixties and early seventies in their fight for open housing and other civil rights had burned out. I could not help but feel that some Flint residents were oblivious to the disparities among the ethnic groups. Maybe, appearing unaware was a coping mechanism and survival trait.

It appeared that the degradation and violation my colleague endured were attempts to further defame my administration. This experience bothered me because I would have liked to believe that he had the highest regard for others and hurting anyone would be an assault on the human spirit. Months later, the ordeal ended with a set aside of the charge. Regrettably, I learned through information forwarded to me from Flint that a chain of events occurred that resurfaced the entire Atlanta charge. He filed a multimillion dollar lawsuit; the set aside was reinstated and unfortunately, he was found guilty. I mourn for him, my family and everyone else who was affected by this quagmire. The memories will haunt me for many years to come. I will, however, continue to pray for all of those who loved and supported me as well as those who sought to destroy me and my career. Every event has a purpose!

When storms arise, I am reminded of the bible scripture, Romans 8:28, "All things worketh together for the good of those who love the Lord and who are called according to God's purpose." What this simply means is when events and circumstances appear in our lives that we did not plan, if we love God and are living our calling according to God's purpose, then these experiences will work for our good.

Although I had hopes of staying long-term in Flint, it was becoming increasingly clear that was not to be. My experience in Flint was something that I would not wish on my worst enemy.

However, the lessons learned will prove invaluable as I continue my journey. I often wondered, and I still do, what is it going to take for Flint to move in another direction and accept its social reality? A former boom town mired in a changing automotive, manufacturing industry, and suffering from nostalgic paralysis cannot seem to make the leap to an educationally focused community. The change and demands of the automotive industry dictate that education is the only way for this city to regain its momentum and return to prosperity. Unfortunately, the advantages provided by a successful automotive industry caused a mentality that crippled the community and created a sense of helplessness and "woe is me" attitude.

The challenges that I faced as school superintendent primarily dealt with shifting a manufacturing community with low educational expectations to embrace the importance of a quality education. Literacy is an essential component to producing a community of critical thinkers who can adapt regardless of the driving forces of the economy.

Flint is known for its strong unions. The Teachers' Union came out strongly against the reform initiatives. Mind you, I met with the union leadership and other community educational partners throughout the district soliciting feedback and gathering data prior to the first draft of the reform plan. It was important to me that I had their input, recognizing that the UTF is a driving force in Flint Community Schools. Yes, in looking back, maybe the roll-out could have been handled in phases; however, the pressure from possible state takeover did not allow for this luxury. The staff that I needed the most to make this challenging time a lot less difficult didn't understand, accept or fully support the expediency with which the changes needed to be made. To the faculty and staff who understood the urgency, need and relevance of an aggressive reform, I thank you. This district had been in a conundrum for many years, and some educators knew the severity of the educational plight of Flint Community Schools and eagerly embraced the changes.

I had no idea that my reform plan would have upset so many adults. As an educator, I was naïve enough to believe that the priority of all educators was preparing our children for greatness. I soon realized that we often talk the talk, but politics inhibit us from walking the walk. It became a stage of saying the right things in public, but sabotaging in private. I inherited a staff, for the most part, that supported the inside candidate. This allegiance became my nemesis. This is not to say I did not have any supporters because there were many; however, I was constantly reminded of the damage that a few can cause. For instance, the Reform Plan called for realignment of secondary schools. Being new to the area, I relied on my staff, many of whom had never left Flint and understood the neighborhood boundaries, to define the schools within the defined boundaries. Mistake! Instant sabotage that caused overcrowded schools, made parents irate and gave politicians a grandstand to place blame. Intellectually, overcrowding should not have occurred in that the district had been losing students annually for many years due to the deteriorating Michigan economy. I found out later, that most of the overcrowding was attributed to many of the staff not understanding "grandfathering."

My Reform Plan became the foundation for all candidates running for the 2007 Board of Education elections. All incumbent Board members who supported me were targets for the other eighteen candidates. Such a large pool of candidates was by design to split the city-wide vote. Out of 90,000 registered voters, only 7,000 voted in this election! All eighteen candidates had one goal in mind–to remove me as Superintendent of Flint Community Schools and return the district to the way "it used to be"–failing. A relative of one of the candidates was so brazen as to tell me, "… and when he wins, he is going to help get rid of you because of all of these painful changes!" It seems that the adults were the primary focus and not the children. Obviously, the candidates had not read the Reform Plan in its entirety to gain an understanding of the long-term goals designed to raise student achievement. Unfortunately, all incumbents up for re-election, except one, lost their Board of Education seats.

It is important to note that although my Reform Plan became the platform for the candidates for the School Board, many components of the Reform Plan were showing, and continue to show, improvements in the students' academic success. Some of these components have been praised by the local media and other educational arenas. It is my desire that Flint will one day return to its richness by continuing to invest in educating children.

Flint, Michigan proved to be my storm, my tornado. As most of you will agree, when the storm clears, there are sometimes blue skies and sunshine. Every event has a purpose!

Gordon Parks once said, "I still dream big at times, but when my dreams pull apart, as they sometimes do, I've learned not to press the panic button."

Chapter Nine

The Value of
Networking

"I have wise advisors ...and I asked them, "Are my goals realistic? Am
I moving in a good direction? Even though I am the one who finally decides
... I require a wide range of opinions."
-Janet Jackson

      The dictionary defines networking as a "supportive system of sharing information and services among individuals and groups." My experience is that networking is more than as defined. It is about building nurturing relationships that are reciprocal and intuitive. I was very fortunate during those tumultuous times in Flint to have my national network of mentors, colleagues and fraternity brothers surrounding and covering me. Some of them understood my plight as they, too, had survived career tornadoes. When all of my "Flint issues" were being covered by the press, many of my colleagues in the educational community restrained themselves from saying "I told you so," while others could not resist. You see, many of them were against my coming to Flint in the first place because of Flint's history of high superintendent-turnover, five superintendents in six years. I realized that it was time to contemplate my exit from Flint Community Schools because I knew that I had to salvage my career and return to the high-standing, impeccable track-record that I had worked so hard to acquire and maintain. My network all sympathized and agreed to make me aware of other superintendent opportunities.

Participating in the many educational and superintendents' associations also provided me with support and a network on a different level: superintendents identifying and relating to other superintendents' challenges and struggles. It was amazing the amount of peer support that I received from other older superintendents and to hear the details of others' career defining moments. Of course, none of the other superintendents had experienced the level of personal attacks that I had!

It was at a conference of one of the professional organizations to which I belonged when I learned of several available superintendent opportunities. My wife and I had many discussions about my experiences in Flint and definite ideas and opinions about the kind of place in which we wanted to educate and rear our children. It was very clear to me what I **did not** want for my future.

There was one opportunity in particular that was most attractive in Central Illinois. As I discussed this opportunity with representatives from the search firm, I remembered the times while driving on Highway 55 in route to St. Louis, Missouri to visit in-laws and commenting to my wife that "I am really intrigued about the Land of Lincoln; one day, we are going to visit the Lincoln Museum and the State's capitol." How ironic that the land of Lincoln presented an opportunity that could possibly restore my faith in community leadership and my commitment to urban education. Every event has a purpose!

Chapter Ten

I Still Believe
In Rainbows

---

*"The beauty of the rainbow reminds us that
the wetness of the rain was worth it."*
-Me

Beyond every dark cloud of fear and doubt, there is a blessing
waiting for us. By enduring storms, I have discovered rainbows.
For those who believe that all hope is gone, I encourage you to
realize that there is a rainbow awaiting you, just be strong.

I began the application process for a couple of the opportunities presented to me, including one in New York, my home state.
After much thought and many more discussions with the representatives of the search firm, my family and I decided that I would

focus on the opportunity in Illinois. The dynamics of this district were more conducive to providing the quality of life that we wanted. In addition, my own research indicated that this particular district valued education and embraced educational excellence.

Once again, I found myself in a fierce battle with a pool of candidates who were highly talented and thirsty for this opportunity. Again, I was selected for the first-round of interviews. As fate would have it, news of my candidacy spread throughout the Flint Community like wild fire! The telephone lines, e-mails and blogs jammed the airwaves with every negative comment that a small group could think of, hoping to thwart my upcoming interview with the Board members. Mind you, some in the Flint Community had made it clear that I was not what Flint wanted and yet when there was a possibility for me to leave, efforts were made to sabotage my ticket out. Psychosis at its utmost! This toxic group referred to me as everything but one of God's children. They were hateful enough to contact Board members and the local media with rants. How low can some people go? Once again, I drew from the strength of my parents and the power of my God, and persevered through another attempt by my detractors to persecute me. I believed that if this group had its way, I would never work again! However, I was determined to stand tall.

Fortunately, the Board members with whom I was to interview did not buy into the drama that some people from Flint were intent on bringing into their space. These Board members were professional, intelligent and wanted no part of a soap opera mentality. They were able to see through the emotion and the lies. The Board members, after all, had done their due diligence. I was selected for a second interview.

During the second interview, I and the other finalist had to present before invited community representatives as to why we should become the new superintendent. My wife accompanied me for the interview. The Board members and the community wanted to also connect with the spouses of the finalists. Included in my presentation were responses to the lies that some from Flint had written in the online blogs. The community asked hard questions, and I held back nothing and answered everything. The final phase of the interview was a dinner with Board members and my wife. Before leaving dinner, we asked, "When will the decision be made?" One Board member responded, "Within forty-eight hours." Later that night, we received the call, and the person on the other end asked, "Is this the new superintendent of District 186?" I had been selected to lead this great district! My wife and I were so overcome with emotions that all we could do was hold each other and cry. Until that moment of emotional release, I had not realized how much we had suppressed our pain. Our path through Flint was coming to an end. Sometimes a rainbow does appear after a storm!

Chapter Eleven

The Journey...

"Never judge a man unless you have walked five miles in his moccasins."

-Western Indian Proverb

It takes courage, commitment, prayer, belief in oneself, humility, confidence and the willingness to not grow weary along the way. Things probably will not happen instantaneously – rather it takes time and energy to produce a product. Unfortunately, many people want a product, but do not want to endure the process.

Life's journey can take many paths and is often covered with detours along the way. My experiences so far have taught me that there really is value in the valley, that there are lessons in all of our experiences. We need only to recognize the lessons and learn from them!

What do you learn when you are experiencing all highs and no lows? Flint was my career low, but the experience was lessons learned that I will never forget. I learned how to survive a storm; no, not just survive, but thrive. I learned that you should be very careful about what you pray for; you just might get it. I learned that the universe does not give one more than he or she can bear. If you remain steadfast, focused and committed to your dreams and principles, you will prevail.

If your journey is leading you to a superintendent's position, I leave with you my Superintendent's Entry Plan, Six Essentials For Highly-Effective Learning Communities and a Literature Review on Parent Involvement. Trust me, these tools have been confirmed, validated and proven to work in high achieving districts! Use them if you dare!

Enjoy peace, prosperity and happiness during your journey. Thank you for allowing me to share a part of mine with you!

Resources

Educational Leadership Resources

A Superintendent's Entry Plan

Walter Milton, Jr. Ed.D.

PURPOSE

I believe that purposeful and intentional planning is a benchmark of effective leadership. I define planning as a set of well thought out ideas and goals to follow that will meet a pre-determined end. I have developed a systematic strategic plan that is purposeful, for taking the helm of leadership as a newly appointed Superintendent of Schools. I believe that this plan is appropriate for any school district, regardless of its status as rural, suburban, or urban; or regardless of the ethnic, educational, or gender backgrounds of the faculty, staff, or students. I have pulled ideas together from several sources to create this document; much of which is built from personal experiences as a newly appointed Principal and Superintendent of Schools.

The following plan includes seven components:
1. Entry Plan Goals and Expected Outcomes
2. Relationship Building with the School Board
3. Central Office Consensus
4. Assessing the Administrative Team
5. Teaming with Teachers for Teaching and Learning
6. Partnering with Parents and Community (Parent and Community Involvement)
7. Development of a 3 to 5 Year Comprehensive District Educational Plan (CDEP)

I: Entry Plan Goals and Expected Outcomes

GOALS	EXPECTED OUTCOMES
1. To get to know the school district and its constituency as fully as possible in a brief period of time, outside the daily context of crisis and problem solving.	• Initial introduction and conversation with all of the district's major stakeholders and groups • Collection of names and contact information of district's collaborative partners: community organizations, government agencies, and local businesses
2. To examine key issues of the school district's past.	• Make sense of district's history and important issues • Identify a pattern of practice, which can affect how the district may function in the future • Make note of practices and historical happenings that have served as a benefit to the district
3. To assess the school district's educational plan and systems for student achievement.	• List effective systems, practices, grants, and programs that result in student achievement • List of tasks and areas of need that will improve student achievement; and rank them in order of priority
4. To make use of collected information to develop long term goals and strategies for accomplishing effective education.	• Development of three to five year strategic educational plan

II: Relationship Building with the School Board

OBJECTIVES	PHASE I STRATEGIES	PHASE II STRATEGIES	PHASE III STRATEGIES
1. To examine the ground rules and procedures which have governed how the BOE has conducted business in the past	• Facilitate strategic planning session with full BOE • Interview each BOE member to obtain specificity of individual's input	• Provide written summary of strategic planning session to full BOE • Interview each BOE member to get individual feedback on results of strategic planning session	• Refer to findings for clarification of a historical context when necessary
2. To develop with the BOE a set of ground rules and procedures which will govern how we operate in the future	• Facilitate strategic planning session with full BOE • Interview each BOE member to obtain specificity of individual's input	• Provide written summary of strategic planning session to full BOE • Interview each BOE member to get individual feedback on results of strategic planning session	• Implement new set of ground rules

II: **Relationship Building with the School Board** *continued*

OBJECTIVES	PHASE I STRATEGIES	PHASE II STRATEGIES	PHASE III STRATEGIES
3. To determine the issues which the BOE believes we should concentrate; and develop a predictable set of tasks/goals in which the Central Office and BOE will work on in the next 3 to 5 years	• Facilitate strategic planning session with full BOE • Interview each BOE member to obtain specificity of individual's input	• Facilitate a prioritizing session with the BOE of the tasks to be accomplished annually, and over the next 3 to 5 years • Develop a work plan to accomplish tasks; including description of tasks, time frame, and individual(s) responsible for completion • Regularly schedule meetings with individual BOE members	• Implement strategies to accomplish completion of tasks • Regularly report out to BOE on progress of tasks completion • Regularly meet with BOE committees to assist in accomplishing tasks • Regularly meet with individual BOE members for guidance and feedback on implementation strategies • Provide *End of the Year Review* report to BOE

III: Central Office Consensus

OBJECTIVES	PHASE I STRATEGIES	PHASE II STRATEGIES	PHASE III STRATEGIES
1. To determine the norms, procedures, and processes which govern how each of the tasks of the Central Office is accomplished	Briefing sessions for the Superintendent conducted with the following Central Office groups: • District Administration (business and finance, human resource, curriculum and intruction, technology, special education, student assessment) • Support Staff (secretaries, clerks, accountants) • Transportation and Buildings and Grounds (responsible leadership) • Document information shared in the briefing session	• Report out to BOE of findings, feedback, and recommendations	• Refer to findings for clarification of a historical context when necessary

III: Central Office Consensus *continued*

OBJECTIVES	PHASE I STRATEGIES	PHASE II STRATEGIES	PHASE III STRATEGIES
2. To develop work plans for the predictable tasks which Central Office staff will undertake within the next year	• Facilitate series of strategic planning session with Central Office staff (conduct them based on grouping if necessary) • Interview individual Central Office staff to obtain clarity of information and to assess practicality of recommended strategies	• Develop a work plan to accomplish tasks; including description of tasks, time frame, and individual(s) responsible for completion	• Share work plan with BOE • Implement plan and schedule regular meetings with Central office staff, and individual meetings with relevant staff to determine progress of plan completion
3. To clarify the role responsibilities of each member of the Central Office	• Conduct individual interviews with each Central Office staff member to obtain first hand information of role responsibilities • Briefing session with leadership responsible for human resources	• Work with relevant Central Office leadership to revise, if necessary, role responsibilities	• Review annually Central Office role responsibilities
4. To consider the reorganization of Central Office functions	• Review district's organizational chart	• Use information from various distric strategic planning sessions to assess and determine need for reorganization of Central Office	• Present understanding and/or recommendations to BOE

IV: Assessing the Administrative Team

OBJECTIVES	PHASE I STRATEGIES	PHASE II STRATEGIES	PHASE III STRATEGIES
1. To clarify the role responsibilities of building administration and how they coordinate with Central Office administration	• Conduct briefing session with building level administration • Conduct individual interviews with building administration to obtain clarity of role responsibilities	• Discuss findings with relevant district level leadership, including director of human resources • Revise role responsibilities if necessary • Require from relevant Central Office staff a calendar of regularly scheduled meetings with building level administration • Develop calendar of regularly scheduled meetings with relevant Central Office staff and building administration	• Document process through meeting minutes and bi-weekly reports
2. To develop work plans for the predictable tasks which building level administration will undertake within the next year	• Facilitate series of strategic planning session with building level administration and relevant Central Office staff • Interview building administration to obtain clarity of information and to assess practicality of recommended strategies	• Develop a work plan to accomplish tasks; including description of tasks, time frame, and individual(s) responsible for completion	• Share work plan with BOE • Implement plan and schedule regular meetings with building administration to determine progress of plan completion

V: Teaming with Teachers for Teaching and Learning

OBJECTIVES	PHASE I STRATEGIES	PHASE II STRATEGIES	PHASE III STRATEGIES
1. To get to know teachers and instructional support staff as fully as possible in a brief period of time.	• Conduct interviews with members of the Teacher Association's leadership (union) • Conduct a series of dinner meetings to meet instructional staff in groups relevant to grade areas (Pre-K to G3, G4-6, G7-8, G9-12)	• Conduct quarterly "district town hall meetings" with instructional staff to share information, give commendations, and answer questions	• Use findings, feedback, and recommendations to develop district wide education plan with the core goal of improving/enriching student achievement (CDEP)
2. To assess the school district's educational plan and systems for student achievement.	• Interview teachers (grade level representatives) to assess knowledge of district's educational plan and strategies for raising student achievement • Conduct a series of teacher focus groups to determine and assess instructional practices, prominent teaching methodologies, curricula, and evidence of literacy based instruction through core content areas	• Document findings of teacher focus groups in Executive Summary Report; and share with all relevant stakeholders (Teachers Association, BOE, district and building administration	

VI: Partnering with Parents and Community (Parent and Community Involvement)

OBJECTIVES	PHASE I STRATEGIES	PHASE II STRATEGIES	PHASE III STRATEGIES
1. To determine the norms, procedures, activities, and programs for parent involvement in the past	• Conduct a series of parent focus groups to gain knowledge of past practices • Interview leadership of parent organizations • Conduct a series of home visits to develop knowledge base of district's families	• Document findings (and any recommendations) in Summary Report; share report with BOE	• Refer to findings for clarification of a historical context when necessary • Use recommendations as part of an annual Parent and Community Involvement work plan
2. To determine the norms, procedures, activities, and programs for community involvement in the past	• Conduct a series of community focus groups to gain knowledge of past practices • Interview leadership of selected community organizations, businesses, and government (seek BOE's guidance)	• Document findings (and any recommendations) in Summary Report; share report with BOE	• Refer to findings for clarification of a historical context when necessary • Use recommendations as part of an annual Parent and Community Involvement work plan

VI: Partnering with Parents and Community *continued*

OBJECTIVES	PHASE I STRATEGIES	PHASE II STRATEGIES	PHASE III STRATEGIES
3. To create an annual Parent and Community Involvement work plan that supports improving/ enriching student achievement	• Conduct a series of focus groups to gain knowledge of pressing issues, and recommendations for improvement • Survey constituency for feedback on strategies	• Use collected data to create an annual Parent and Community Involvement work plan; including goals, tasks, time frame, and persons responsible for tasks completion	• Share work plan with BOE • Implement plan and schedule regular meetings with leadership of parent organizations; and relevant community representatives

VII: Development of Three to Five Year Comprehensive District Education Plan (CDEP)

OBJECTIVES	PHASE I STRATEGIES	PHASE II STRATEGIES	PHASE III STRATEGIES
1. To make use of collected information to develop long term goals and strategies for accomplishing effective education.	• Using information and data documented and collected from strategies implemented in components 1-6, work with relevant Central Office administrative staff to for mulate information into a Comprehensive District Educational Plan (CDEP) [The core goal of CDEP should be raising or enriching student achievement]	• Publish and share CDEP with all stakeholders (BOE, administration, teachers and instructional support, parents, students, community representatives, others)	• Implement CDEP • Annually review and assess accomplishment of tasks and strategies

Six Essential Components for Highly Effective K-12 Learning Communities

1. Valid and Reliable Assessment	2. Scientifically Based and Researched Curriculum and Instruction	3. Sustained Professional Development
• Informs and guides all educational and instructional decisions • Holds all stakeholders accountable, beginning with the leadership at the top • Informs all stakeholders on the "teaching and learning gaps" and "comprehensive educational systems gaps"	• Focused on what students are expected to know and demonstrate; as determined by state standards • Include strategies that are systematic, explicit, and based on the latest research and milestones • Is culturally relevant and responsive to all students • Include literacy skills development as a core component of the learning process • Provides intensive "time on task" in four core learning areas: English Language Arts, Math, Science, and Social Studies	• Builds teachers' skills capacity in relevant content areas • Builds skills for all teachers in scientifically based reading research • Is ongoing and provide several opportunities for onsite technical assistance and modeling • Expands teachers' skills in literacy based instruction, classroom management, student-centered instruction, culturally relevant and responsive instruction, and differentiated instruction

Six Essential Components for Highly Effective K-12 Learning Communities
continued

4. Capable Leadership	5. Responsible Fiscal Management	6. Parent Involvement and Community Relations
• Is dynamic, strong, and actively committed to improving student achievement • Is competent and demonstrates a love for learning • Supervises through coaching, consensus building, and support • Models the best practices of the profession both academically and professionally	• Appropriately wrapping the lion's share of school dollars around student achievement • Budget outlines demonstrating what is best for children • Competent and responsible stewardship of resources allocated to the school district • Keen awareness of budgetary process to ensure teachers and students are provided the necessary resources for success	• Including parents as a central role in student learning • Helping parents build skills that will assist them in propelling their children toward academic and social success • Giving students several opportunities to participate in community activities and events that demonstrate academic and social excellence • Giving students several opportunities to connect with local, state, and national persons of excellence

The district-wide needs assessment would include, but not be limited to the *following essential components and evaluative elements:*

1. Valid and Reliable Assessment

Evaluative Elements
- District's systems for assessing student achievement
- District's assessment accountability measures
- Evaluation plans/tools for assessing the District's systems for raising student achievement
- District's systems for student retention, and reduction of student drop out rate

2. Scientifically Based and Researched (SBR) Curriculum and Instruction

Evaluative Elements
- District's instructional systems for teaching and learning Reading and Writing throughout the curricula
- District's instructional systems for teaching and learning in the four core academic areas: English Language Arts, Math, Social Studies, and Science
- District's instructional systems for intervention services to students who are "high risk" and "some risk" for not meeting state standards
- District's instructional systems for English Language Learners (ELL)

3. Sustained Professional Development

Evaluative Elements

- District's current professional development plan for instructional staff, non-instructional staff, building level administration, and district level administration
- District's current professional development plan's connectedness to SBR teaching and learning, and NCLB requirements

4. Capable Leadership

Evaluative Elements

- District's current organizational structure and its effectiveness in raising student achievement
- District's staffing patterns for classroom teachers, instructional specialists, grant funded programs, extra curricula activities that impact student achievement, building level leadership, district level leadership, and support staff
- Roles and responsibilities of all district personnel that connects to student achievement

5. Fiscal Responsibility

Evaluative Elements

- District's current financial status and competence
- Fiscal systems that connect the District's dollars to student achievement (ways in which dollars are wrapped around instruction and classroom services)
- Fiscal systems that link to transportation, technology, facilities and grounds
- Fiscal evaluation plans/tools for measuring fiscal competence, sustainable funding, and financial projections
- Fiscal checks and balances that prevent over spending and encourage opportunities for savings

6. Parent Involvement and Community Relations

Evaluative Elements

- District's current systems and programs for involving parents in the teaching and learning process
- District's current community, business, and government relationships through special programs, funding, or in-kind services

LITERATURE REVIEW: PARENT INVOLVEMENT

This literature review summarizes some of the key studies and reviews the present knowledge about parent involvement and its effect on the student's educational endeavors. The literature review is divided into six parts. The first part provides an overview of parental involvement. The second part includes information on the models and types of parental involvement. The third part focuses on Epstein's theoretical framework. The fourth part deals with parental involvement and academic success. The fifth part investigates benefits and barriers to parental involvement, and the sixth part deals with enhancing parental involvement.

Historical Overview of Parental Involvement

Parent involvement and parent education today had their roots in parent involvement and parent education of yesterday. According to Gordon (1977), formalized parent education initiatives date back to biblical times and probably began when early civilizations passed parenting skills from generation to generation. Parents had always been their children's first teachers. The history of modern parent education can be traced from Pestalozzi's (1915) *How Gertrude Teaches Her Children.* Parent education classes were first held in Portland, Maine as early as 1815. Classes usually consisted of middle-class religious mothers of Protestant Calvinist groups who gathered together to learn how to discipline and break the will of children (Thornburg, 1991).

The three theories on child rearing that were evident in the United States in the nineteenth century were based on European lines of thought. The first theory was the Calvinist doctrine of infant depravity that required strict guidance by the parents and obedience by the child. According to Brim (1965), the Calvinist doctrine stated that a willful child reflected evil from within. To spare the rod was to spoil the child.

The second child rearing theory in the United States stemmed from the influence of Rousseau, Pestalozzi, and Froebel who viewed children as basically good. Rousseau's influence on Pestalozzi was evident and when Froebel studied under Pestalozzi, he was greatly influenced by Pestalozzi's belief in the natural goodness of children. The family's care was important. "Thus maternal instinct and love gradually introduced the child to his little outside world, proceeding from the whole to the part, from the near to the remote" (Froebel, 1887, p. 66).

Froebel's kindergartens were brought to the United States by Margarethe Schurz, a prominent German immigrant; Elizabeth Peabody, a kindergarten advocate and sister-in-law of Horace Mann; and Henry Barnard, Secretary of the Connecticut Board of Education and later Commissioner of Education. Each promoted the Froebian kindergarten movement throughout the United States. Since Froebel felt that parents were an integral component of early education, the kindergarten movement carried the tradition of involving parents. Subsequently, the decade between the 1870s and the 1880s saw an increase in parent involvement (Berger, 1991).

A third theoretical view of child reading implemented in the United States was derived from the work of John Locke. He viewed children as influenced by the environment; therefore, he asserted that education interventions were necessary. As immigrants who were different from earlier settlers arrived in the United

States, Locke's concept reasserted itself (Berger, 1991).

Then, the explosion of 26 major parent programs heralded the decade of the 1920s. The need to "mainstream" lessened because restrictive legislation had reduced the number of immigrants arriving in the United States. Most of the parent education groups were not established for new arrivals; they met in groups for their own needs. Middle-class parent formed groups for study enlightenment or, in some cases, they were developed in response to a need for health information about tuberculosis or nutrition. Many parent cooperatives were established in five locations across the nation, and PTA membership grew from 190,000 in 1920 to nearly 1,500,000 in 1930. The Child Study Association of America (CSAA) sponsored the first parent education university course at Columbia University in 1920. This association grew from 56 parent groups to 135 in 1927 (Whipple, 1929). Continued growth in preschool and parent education flourished on many fronts (Berger, 1991).

In response to the need for a course of study, Gruenberg (1927) published the *Outline of Child Study: A Manual for Parents and Teachers*, a textbook used as a study guide for parent education groups. The guide offered information on child development including issues such as speech development, heredity, obedience, freedom and discipline, mental tests, and emotional and intellectual development. Special problems of adolescence were addressed and readers were provided with an outline and references. The emergence of study groups, curriculum guides, and the formation in 1925 of the National Council of Parent Education demonstrated the importance accorded to parent education during this period. The council continued until 1928, using its influence to establish parent programs through federal agencies, conference leadership, and advice to establish parent education groups (Brim, 1965; Gruenberg, 1940). Whipple's (1929) *Twenty-eighth Yearbook: National Society for the Study of Education* was devoted to preschool and parent education. Berger (1991) stated that the financial crash of 1929 brought a change for many families in the United States, and although the parent education movement was reduced, it continued through federal and state support.

During the 1930s, the White House Conference on Child Health and Protection, held in November, was attended by over 4,000 specialists who recommended various associations, organizations, and educational departments of different states be requested to study the possibilities for organizing parent education as part of the system of public instruction and that professional groups and civic organizations concerned with children be asked to study their opportunities and obligations for parent education (Gordon, 1977). According to Berger (1991), these objectives of child rearing and parental involvement were reminiscent of the mainstreaming of earlier days, with the intent of mainstreaming not only immigrants but "our indigent poor, the immigrant waves from the farm to the city represented by the movement of southern Blacks, the immigration of Puerto Ricans to New York and other urban centers, the Chicano in the southwestern United States, and the Appalachian poor" (p. 209).

Social and economic conditions of the 1930s affected families and children. 0Agencies were established to help families survive during the depression. The Works Progress Administration (WPA) offered a forum for parents to learn about home management practices. The Federal Emergency Relief Administration

(FERA) allowed work-relief wages for unemployed teachers to organize and direct nursery schools. The FERA intended to have schools take over nursery school programs, which would become a permanent and integral part of the public school program (Davies, 1987).

Although the nation was consumed by World War II during the first half of the 1940s, parent education continued and child care services were provided to allow mothers to work in war efforts. Child-rearing practices changed radically from the 1920s and 1930s. The be-tough with them, feed-on-schedule, and let them cry-it-out doctrines were closed and complete. The emotional and social health of children was recognized as important, particularly since many young recruits had been unable to serve during World War II because of mental health (Brim, 1965).

The era of the 1950s was considered the baby boom era. World War II was over; families were able to proceed with their lives; and emphasis was on the family. In the late 1950s, factories introduced robots, computers, and other machines as part of a self-operating system called automation. Automation gave rise to many displaced workers causing a feeling of non-accomplishment. Teaching machines were introduced to education (Schmidt, 1991). Benjamin Spock's (1957) *The Common Sense Book of Baby and Child Care* was written to help parents who were encouraged to allow children's self-regulation. Erickson's Child and Society, first published in 1950, analyzed the eight stages of man. He emphasized the first four stages of childhood: trust vs. mistrust, autonomy vs. shame and doubt, initiative vs. guilt, and industry vs. inferiority. Erickson presented the view that children needed a nurturing early life in order to achieve the necessary mental health to develop trust, autonomy, initiative, and industry (Erickson, 1960).

Models of Parental Involvement

Current models of parental involvement will be described with a focus on Epstein's six types of involvement.

Haynes and Ben-Avie (1996) categorize parental involvement using a three-tier model: (a) General participation, (b) helping in the classroom or sponsoring and supporting school programs, and (c) parent participation on the School Planning and Management Team.

Eccles and Harold (1996) have developed five variables of parental involvement: Monitor (parent responses to teacher requests and information), Volunteer (parent participation in volunteer activities at school), Involvement (parent involvement with the child's daily activities), Progress (parent contact with the school about the child's progress), and Extra Help (parent contact with the school about how to give extra help).

Gordon and Breivogel (1976) suggested **six types of parent involvement:**

1. The first was thought of as the traditional type of parent involvement, namely parent as audience or bystander-observer. This parent-as-audience was the passive way in which schools usually involved parents. An example of this would be parents attending an open house at their child's school.

2. A second way of involving parents was as decision makers. This happened when parents volunteered for parent teacher organizations or school advisory councils and made decisions related to their child's school.

3. A third type of parent involvement was shown when the parent began working in the classroom as a volunteer. Bringing parents into schools as volunteers and aides influenced the school as much as parents were influenced.

4. In the fourth type of parent involvement, the parent was involved in the classroom as a paid paraprofessional or teacher's aide.

5. The parent as a learner was the fifth type of parent involvement. This occurred when parents took a class in child development or parenting.

6. Finally, the sixth way to involve parents was as a teacher of his or her own child. (pp. 18-19)

Epstein's Framework

Epstein's (1995) framework includes the following six patterns or typologies of involvement that help families and schools fulfill their shared responsibilities for children's learning and development: (a) parenting, (b) communicating, (c) volunteering, (d) learning at home, (e) decision making, and (f) collaboration with the community. Epstein's framework of six types of involvement, derived from data about school programs, directed attention to practices that fall within the areas of family-school-community interactions. The typology helped educators locate where they were starting from in their present practices, plan more comprehensive programs, and monitor progress in school, family, and community connections. The framework also helped researchers to locate questions and report results in ways that may form and improve practices.

Type 1 Parenting

The first pattern in Epstein's framework involves parenting which includes assisting families with parenting skills and setting home conditions to support children as students, as well as, assisting schools to understand families. Epstein (1996) identified as a challenge for schools the necessity of developing a wider view of communication that includes making information available in a variety of forms so all parents can access it in a variety of ways and at a variety of times. She contended that families were responsible for providing for children's health, preparing children for school, teaching practical life skills, and building positive home conditions which supported learning and behavior expectations. Strategies include workshops, videotapes, computerized telephone messages on parenting and child rearing, courses for training parents, family support programs to assist families with health, nutrition, and other services, and home visits at transition points to preschool, elementary, middle, and high school as well as neighborhood meetings to help families understand schools and to help schools understand families.

The effect of "parenting" for parents is (a) a better understanding of and confidence about parenting, child and adolescent development, and changes in home conditions for learning as children transition through school; and (b) a feeling of support from school and other parents. The effect of "parenting" for teachers is (a) an understanding of families' backgrounds, cultures, concerns, goals, needs, and views of children; (b) a respect for families' strengths and efforts, and (c) an understanding of student diversity (Epstein, Coates, Salinas, Sanders, & Simon, 1997).

Type 2 Communicating

According to Epstein (1992), this typology refers to the basic obligations of schools to communicate with families regarding school programs and student progress through effective school-to-home and home-to-school communications. "Communicating" with families can take many forms. Report cards, newsletters, telephone conversations, and open houses are some of the traditional ways schools communicate. Schools that varied their form and frequency of their communications with parents best met the needs of families. Challenges in this area include making sure communications from the school to home are clear and understandable for all parents Factors such as parents who do not speak English, have poor sight and need large print or "who do not read well" need to be addressed (Epstein, 1995).

Epstein (1995) reports with effective communication, parents understand school programs and policies. Through monitoring their child's progress, parents are able to respond effectively to problems. Teachers gain an increased diversity and rise of communications with families and an awareness of a teacher's own ability to communicate clearly (Epstein, 2001; Epstein et al., 1997).

Type 3 Volunteering

"Volunteering" involves organizing volunteers and audiences to support the school and students and providing volunteer opportunities in various locations and at various times. Activities include volunteers in school or classrooms that assist administrators, teachers, and students by tutoring, coaching, lecturing, and chaperoning. They also include volunteers as members of audiences at assemblies, performances, sports events, recognition and award ceremonies, and celebrations (Epstein, 2001).

According to Epstein (1995), parents gain an understanding of the teacher's job, increased comfort with the school, and carry-over of school activities at home. Parents increase their own self-confidence about their ability to work in the school and with children or to take steps to improve their own education as well as gain awareness that families are welcomed and valued. Teachers benefit from a greater awareness of parents' talents and interests in school and children along with greater individual attention to students (Epstein, 1995).

Type 4 Learning at Home

Epstein (2001) states that this typology involves families with their children in homework, goal setting, and other curriculum-related activities and decisions. Epstein defined this type of involvement as teachers helping parents to monitor and assist in their children's learning at home. She contended that it is the responsibility of the school to enable families to understand how to help their children at home. Teachers should assist parents in how to interact with their children on activities coordinated with the school's curriculum or activities designed to enrich learning. Epstein's research and other research report that this type of parent involvement was closely related to student academic achievement (Ames, Stefano, Watkins, & Sheldon, 1995; Connors-Tadros, 1995; Epstein & Connors, 1994; Salganik, 1994). Activities include (a) information for families on skills required for students in all subjects at each grade level; (b) information on homework policies; and (c) information on how to assist students to improve skills on various class and school assessments (Epstein, 2001; Swap, 1993).

Parents benefit by gaining knowledge on how to support, encourage, and help their child at home. Teachers gain an increased respect for family time, and satisfaction with family involvement and support (Epstein, 2001). Teachers also recognize the helpfulness of single-parent, dual-income, and less formally educated families in motivating and reinforcing student learning. Teachers become aware of the need to clarify their expectations about homework and to provide assistance and resources to parents to enable them to assist their students at home (Moles & D'Angelo, 1983; Swap, 1993; Turnbull & Turnbull, 1990).

Type 5 Decision Making

Involvement in decision making, governance, and advocacy constituted the fifth type of involvement of Epstein's model. Decision-making activities include families as participants in school decisions and developing parent leaders and representatives. Activities such as PTA/PTO, school councils, improvement teams, committees and other school-based or independent parent organizations prepare parents for leadership roles and assist parent representatives to obtain information from and give information to the families that they represent (Epstein, 2001). Schools assisted in this area by training parents to be leaders and involving them in the decision-making process (Epstein, 1987, 1996).

Parents gain a feeling of ownership of the school. They

become more aware of school, district, and state policies; they also benefit from shared experiences and connections with other families (Epstein, 1995; Swap, 1993). Epstein (1995) redefines decision making to mean real, shared decision making in partnerships that are not power struggles but work toward shared goals. Teachers gain an awareness of parent perspectives as a factor in policy development and decisions as well as viewing family members as having equal status as representatives on committees and in leadership roles. Teachers also benefit by using teachers' knowledge to help them select among curricular options or develop further options (Epstein, 2001).

Type 6 Collaborating with the Community

According to Epstein (2001), this typology includes coordinating resources and services from the community for families, students, and the school, and providing services to the community. Collaborating with the community challenges schools to build partnerships that match school goals and develop opportunities for all families to be involved in community programs.

Collaborating with the community includes recognizing the learning activities that take place in the community. Club and volunteer work should be valued as learning experiences (Epstein, 2001).

Parents benefit by gaining knowledge and use of local resources to improve health, increase skills, develop talents, and obtain needed services for the family. Teachers benefit from an increasing awareness of community resources to enrich curriculum and instruction. Teachers gain openness to and skills in using mentors, business partners, community volunteers, and others to assist students and augment teaching practices (Epstein, 2001).

This type of involvement opened a relatively unexplored research agenda. It was not part of the research that produced the theoretical model for which Epstein was most recognized. Each type of involvement can be fulfilled by many different practices of partnership. Each type had particular challenges that must be met to have a successful program that engages all families. Each type suggested needed re-definitions of some basic principles of involvement to succeed with today's families. Finally, each type was likely to lead to different results for students, for parents, and for teaching practice and for school climate. Although all schools could use this framework of the six types as a guide, each school must tailor its choice of practices to meet the needs of families and students at various grade levels (Epstein, 1996).

According to Epstein's (1996) theoretical model, these six types of parent involvement and participation practices interacted to form the framework for a comprehensive program guided by three goals: (a) to improve school programs, classroom management, and teacher effectiveness, (b) to improve student learning and development, and (c) to improve parents' awareness of their role in children's educational, social, and personal development across the school years.

According to Epstein (1996), from her own studies and work with many schools, districts, and states, and from her new knowledge researched by the Center on Families, Communities, Schools and Children's Learning, they had developed, tested, and applied the theory of overlapping influences and used the framework of six types of involvement to help schools establish and maintain a comprehensive program of partnership with families and communities.

Parental Involvement and Academic Success

The effectiveness of education has traditionally been measured by children's academic performance. One of the earliest studies to examine school, teacher, and family variables associated with achievement was the Coleman Report, Equality of Educational Opportunity (Coleman et al., 1966). Some researchers challenged the Coleman study. Mosteller and Moynihan (1972) reanalyzed this report and found that approximately one-half to two-thirds of the studied student variance in achievement was accounted for not by school variables but by home variables, especially socioeconomic status.

Walberg's (1984) synthesis of 2,575 empirical studies of productive factors in learning concluded that educators must consider powerful out-of-school factors, especially the home environment as "the alterable curriculum of the home is twice as predictive of academic learning as is family socioeconomic status" (p. 25). This curriculum includes (a) informed parent-child conversations about everyday and school events, (b) encouragement and discussion of leisure reading, (c) monitoring of television viewing and peer activities, (d) expressed interest in children's academic and personal growth, and (e) delay of immediate gratification to accomplish long-term goals.

Uguroglu and Walberg (1986) and Wang, Haertel, and Walberg (1993) provided additional support for the importance of home environmental variables in school learning in their investigations. These variables encompass not only educational characteristics of the home but also the parental activities and attitudes that support student learning.

Parent involvement has been shown to improve student achievement. In particular, children's academic achievement is more strongly related to their parents' level of involvement in their child's education than to their parents' level of education or income (Singh, Trivette, Keith, & Zill, 1995).

Greenwood and Hickman (1991) reported positive outcomes in their review of family involvement research. These included (a) higher academic achievement for students, (b) a student's sense of well being, (c) improved attendance, (d) improved student and parent perceptions of classroom and school climate, (e) positive student behavior and attitudes, (f) student readiness to do homework, (g) increased student time with parents, (h) better grades, (i) higher educational aspirations, and (j) parent satisfaction with teachers. They concluded that the most effective educational program would be one in which the home and school collaborated and worked together on behalf of the child.

Moles (1982) summarized research findings on the effectiveness of 28 urban home-school partnership programs aimed at poorly educated and low-income parents. These programs used various methods to involve parents including individual conferences, workshops, home visits, and telephone calls. They also supported the parents in home tutoring and educational planning. Overall results indicated the programs were effective with reported reductions in absenteeism, higher achievement scores, and improved behavior. The reviewed research provided findings regarding the effects of parent involvement on achievement and attitudes, presented information on the forms parent involvement takes, identified barriers to home-school collaboration, and presented effective teacher practices for engaging participation.

Finn (1998) suggested that parental involvement in schooling could lead to real academic benefits for children. Four types of at-home parental engagement were consistently associated with school performance: actively organizing and monitoring children's time, helping with homework, discussing school matters with children, and promoting reading activities. Many research findings have shown that specific parenting practices are related to students' academic achievement. Specifically, the home environment has been found to be the most important influence on academic success. They assert that educational stimulation by parents in the home can account for as much as 50% of the difference in grades and test scores among students (Wang, Haertel, & Walberg, 1993). According to the U.S. Department of Education (1994), children's learning and behavior are enhanced when families (a) read together, (b) use television wisely, (c) establish a daily routine, (d) schedule daily homework times, (e) monitor out-of-school activities, (f) talk with their children, (g) communicate positive values, and (h) express high expectations and offer praise and encouragement for achievement.

Keith et al. (1993) conducted a study using eighth-grade subjects from the National Education Longitudinal Study of 1988 to determine if earlier findings would hold for middle-school students and if the influence of parent involvement would be reflected, not only in students' school grades, but in their achievement on standardized tests. The results of this investigation indicated that parent involvement exerts a powerful effect on the achievement of middle-school students and that this influence is independent of family background effects. The effect of parent involvement crossed all academic areas and positively impacted student performance on standardized tests. The findings also suggested that parental involvement and academic achievement may have reciprocal effects on each other, leading the researchers to note "…it appears that higher academic performance results in greater achievement, which in turn, leads to still higher academic performance" (p. 490).

Henderson and Berla (1994) found that parents involved in their children's academic life had a positive effect on the child's ability to learn. Involved parents instilled in their children an appreciation for learning that could last a lifetime. Their research found that "when parents are involved, students achieve more" (p. 7). More importantly, Henderson and Berla found that the most accurate predictor of a student's achievement in school was the extent to which the student's family was able to (a) create a home environment that encouraged learning, (b) communicate high, yet reasonable expectations for their children's achievement and future careers, and (c) become involved in their children's education at school and in the community.

A number of researchers (Beecher, 1984; Henderson, 1987; U.S. Department of Education, 1994) agree that parent involvement improves learning at all grade levels and at all levels of income. There was consensus that all forms of parent involvement strategies seem to be useful but those that are well-planned and more comprehensive, offer more types of roles for parents to play, and occur over a period of time are more effective in raising student achievement.

Not all research supports parental involvement as a powerful indicator of academic success. Baker and Soden (1997) state that methodological limitations compromise even the most promising findings. They reviewed over 200 articles on parent involvement. Many studies examined were judged to be methodologically flawed or failed to present evidence of larger effect size for parent involvement components. Several causal model investigations of parental involvement and academic success have found that direct parental involvement has little, none, or negative effects on the achievement of high school students (Anderson, 1991; Keith, Reimers, Fehrman, Pottebaum, & Aubrey, 1986; Natriello & McDill, 1986).

Enhancing Parental Involvement

Roehlkepartain and Benson (1994) suggested ways of increasing parent involvement by: (a) customizing programs to meet individual community needs, (b) overcoming logistical obstacles such as scheduling and child care, and (c) initiating new practices to build better family-school partnerships. Epstein (1996) established that school practices greatly influence parent involvement. At all grade levels (elementary, middle, and high school), surveys of parents, teachers, principals, and students revealed that if schools invest in practices to involve parents, then parents respond by conducting those practices (Dauber & Epstein, 1989, 1993; Epstein, 1996).

To help promote parent involvement, the National Parent Teacher Association (PTA) has issued six standards:

Standard I: Communication - Communication between home

and school is regular, two-way, and meaningful.

Standard II: Parenting - Parenting skills are promoted and supported.

Standard III: Student Learning - Parents play an integral role in assisting student learning.

Standard IV: Volunteering - Parents are welcome in the school, and their support and assistance are sought.

Standard V: School Decision Making and Advocacy - Parents are full partners in the decisions that affect children and families.

Standard VI: Collaborating with Community - Community resources are used to strengthen schools, families, and student learning (National PTA, 1998).

Benefits of Involving Parents in the Schools

Sui-Chu and Willms (1996) studied eighth-grade students and their parents using National Educational Longitudinal Study (NELS) data. They found that children whose parents regularly discuss their schoolwork and school experience perform better academically than children who rarely discuss school with their parents.

In an examination of the influence of parental involvement on the academic learning of eighth-grade students, Keith, Bickley, Keith, Singh, Trivette, and Troutman (1993) suggested that parental involvement in students' academic lives has a powerful influence on student achievement across all academic areas. Parents' and students' responses were studied under four categories: educational aspirations, parent-child communication, amount of home structure, and participation in school activities.

Rumberger (1990) suggests that there is a relationship between parental involvement and high school dropout rates. His findings indicated that dropouts reported that their parents rarely attended school events or helped them with homework. These parents were more likely to respond to poor grades with punishment, and students rarely consulted their parents when making educational decisions.

Epstein (1996) reported that when teachers were committed to parent involvement, the parents felt that they should help their children, understood more about the curriculum, were more positive about the teachers' interpersonal skills, and rated the overall teaching ability of teachers higher.

Natriello and McDill (1986) examined the determinants of student effort on homework (teachers', parents' and students' standards). The results indicated that teachers', parents' and students' standards all had positive and significant effects on the time spent doing homework.

When schools work with families to support student learning, children tend to succeed not just in school but throughout life (Barclay & Boone, 1997; Henderson & Berla, 1994; Sanders, 1998). High levels of parent involvement yields positive attitudes toward school, greater consistency between family and school goals, better attendance, higher achievement, higher quality homework, higher graduation rates, and greater enrollment in postsecondary education (Epstein, 1991; Epstein & Dauber, 1991).

Barriers Which Exist Toward Parental Involvement

Barriers to parental involvement can be divided into five categories: school environment, culture and language, educational level of parents, psychological issues, and logistical issues. According to Chavkin (1993), parents may feel unwelcome in the school for a variety of reasons. Epstein (1990) concludes that almost all parents from all backgrounds care about their children's education. Yet, so few of them know what schools expect from them or how they might contribute to their children's education. This lack of knowledge acts as a barrier to the establishment of high levels of parental involvement. Epstein (1985) indicated that the majority of teachers have little or no training on working with parents. This, too, is a barrier to high levels of parental involvement.

Moles and D'Angelo (1993) state that some parents are intimidated by educational jargon, which impedes communication between them and teachers. The limited educational background of parents and their own negative school experiences are also factors which affect parent-school relationships (Carrasquillo & London, 1993; Chavkin, 1989; Sui-Chu & Willms, 1996). Transportation, safety and childcare issues influence participation in the school. Cultural diversity affects parental involvement. Some parents may not understand written English. Cultural expectations may be different for immigrant families (Lewis & Henderson, 1997; Moles & D'Angelo, 1993; Swap, 1990).

An issue that Latino parents have in seeking to become involved in their children's education is language (Chavkin & Gonzalez, 1995; Hyslop, 2000). They are not able to understand what is being said or help with homework.

Perceived Barriers for African-American and Hispanic Parental Involvement In Urban Public Schools

In many urban school districts across America, parental involvement is low as it pertains to open house, parent-teacher conferences, curriculum meeting nights, parent teacher organizational meetings, and other after-school activities. This pattern is significant in many low-income, low socioeconomic schools in urban school districts. Often, many of these parents may have had negative incidents throughout their own educational experiences (Gartrell-Nadine, 1995).

Comer (1989) made three compelling arguments. First, parents have knowledge of their children and a relationship upon which school personnel can build. Second, the presence of parents is an essential component to improving accountability and meshing school programs to community needs. Finally, if parents are involved with school programs, they will possibly develop a greater interest in program outcomes and will be supportive of budgetary and political issues. Many African-American parents who have children in urban school districts are made to feel helpless by the ways in which schools present problems to them, or even the way they are invited to schools. For these parents, school is not a safe and friendly environment, and even more disturbing is the fact that their children are not having positive experiences either. In some cases, these parents may feel denigrated by the way in which schools communicate with them. Therefore, as parents, they may be less inclined to visit their children's school or remain involved in the student's academic process or both (Comer, 1989).

Often, language or cultural barriers or both prevent parents from feeling confident in their own ability to collaborate with schools and assist in their children's academic achievement. Below is a summary from the literature of the primary barriers that can impede full parent participation in the educational system (Epstein & Dauber, 1991; Inger, 1992). Knowledge and understanding of the following barriers is the first step toward bridging them.

1. *Language skills:* Inability to understand the language of the school is a major detriment to the African-American parents who have not achieved full English proficiency. When parents do not understand educational jargon or the way information is communicated to them, interactions with the schools are difficult and, therefore, practically nonexistent (Inger, 1992).

2. *Home/school partnerships:* With many African-American and Hispanic parents, teaming with school is not a tradition. Education has historically been perceived as the responsibility of the schools, and parent intervention is viewed as interference with what trained professionals are supposed to do (Gariulo & Graves, 1991).

3. *Work interference:* Work is the major reason stated by parents for noninvolvement in school activities. Conflicts between parent and school schedules may mean parents cannot attend school events, help their children with homework, or in other ways become active participants in their children's education (Epstein, 1995).

4. *Knowledge of the school system:* Many low-income parents and mi-

nority parents view schools as an incomprehensible and purposefully exclusionary system. Lack of trust is often the result of misunderstanding the perceived intentions of each party. Sending home vague and only English communications and scheduling meetings at times when parents cannot attend serve to reinforce parent apprehension. The lack of involvement that results from mistrust and apprehension is often misperceived by schools as a lack of concern for the children's education (Bermudez & Marquez, 1996; Hamilton-Lee, 1988).

5. *Self-confidence:* Many African-American, Hispanic and non-English speaking parents believe that their participation does not help schools perform their jobs as educational institutions; as a result they separate themselves from the process. Parents who feel uncomfortable in the school setting are less likely to be involved than those who have developed a sense of equal partnership (Gargiulo & Graves, 1991).

6. *Past experience:* In some cases, these parents have become victims of racial and linguistic discrimination by schools. Negative feelings toward home-school interaction are often reinforced when schools communicate with parents only to share bad news about their children (Delgado-Gaitan, 1991).

An interesting paradox is that many African-American parents see education as a tool to liberate their children from an impoverished situation, which they and their children may be currently facing (Lomotey, 1989). These parents would be the first to contend that education is important. Parents are the principal educators of their children. However, once children enter school, parents share their responsibilities with educators. Although many African-American parents maintain the ultimate authority for their children's learning, many times these parents do not exercise this authority, given the way they are often received by schools (Lomotey, 1989).

Teacher and Parent Perceptions

Assessing the perceptions held by parents and educators can document some of the barriers to parental involvement. Teachers' ratings of parental involvement may be influenced by their perceptions of the child's achievement and classroom behavior. Parents' perceptions may reflect their assessment of their awareness and evaluation of communications from the school.

Epstein (1995) indicates there are many reasons for developing school, family, and community partnerships. Such partnerships improve school programs and school climate, provide family services and support, and increase parents' skills and leadership, connect families with others in the school and in the community, and help teachers with their work. However, a primary reason to create such partnerships was to help youngsters succeed in school and in later life. When parents, teachers, and students, and others view each other as partners in education, a caring community forms around students and begins its work. Policies and guidelines alone would not be successful without a theory and a framework of basic components of school, family, and community working together.

In a qualitative study of family partnerships in Rhode Island middle schools, Bowen (2003) found that teachers, family members, and students reported similar perceptions of school and family partnerships. All three groups mentioned home-school communication, involvement at school as volunteers/audience, and involvement in learning activities at home most frequently. The remaining three activities in Epstein's topology were ranked by parents, teachers, and students in the same descending order, decision making, parenting, and collaborating with the community.

Hill (2003) investigated the relationship between elementary students' teacher and parent perceptions of parental involvement as it relates to parenting, communicating, volunteering, learning at home, decision making, and collaborating with the community. Results indicated a statistically significant difference between the two types of participants (teacher, parent) on the six dependent variables. Four of the six differences were statistically significant: parenting, communicating, volunteering, and learning at home. Also, where there were significant differences, parents' perceptions were stronger than teachers' perceptions except for collaborating with the community.

Vandergrift and Green (1992) agreed that parent involvement could mean different things, depending upon one's perspective. Some teachers wanted parental involvement in the form of parents helping their children with their homework. Parent involvement can and does take on many forms in the schools. Parental involvement could be reading to preschool children, getting children ready for school every morning, serving as volunteers in the school, serving on collaborative decision-making teams, and lobbying legislatures to become advocates for children.

Evans-Schilling (1996) stated that parent involvement might be facilitated if relationships between parents and teachers become a true partnership based on mutual sharing, helping, and accountability. He contended that as long as schools see the parents' role as only one of background support, for instance providing food, clothing, and shelter, the current relationship between parent and teachers will remain unequal and based on the differential assumptions of power.

Boone (2002) assessed school-level outcomes of a three year statewide family-school partnership initiative in Ohio using the Family-School Connections Survey. Participating schools were located across the state of Ohio and varied in socioeconomic regions. A total of 4,429 surveys were mailed to 17 high schools, 20 middle schools, and a random sample of 29 elementary schools. Schools that were committed to their partnership planning and evaluation for three years were perceived more favorably by staff and parents than first- and second-year schools. Elementary and middle schools were both viewed more favorably by parents and staff than high schools. The level of poverty of a school community was not a significant indicator of differences in the parent and staff feelings associated with the school. Parents and staff of schools in urban settings with very high to average poverty consistently regarded their schools more positively than parents and staff of schools in the other typographical contexts. Urban schools with average to high poverty implemented more partnership opportunities than school in other contexts. Boone's Family-School Connections Survey was used in the current study.

Summary

The review of literature provided a brief historical overview of parental involvement and focused on the following areas:

models of parental involvement, Epstein's framework, parental involvement and academic success, enhancing parental involvement, benefits of involving parents in the school, barriers which exist toward parental involvement, perceived barriers for African-American and Hispanic involvement in urban public schools, and teacher and parent perceptions.

Over 30 years of research has proven that effectively engaging parents and families in the education of their children has the potential to be a significant factor in education reform. Research confirms that regardless of the economic, racial, or cultural background of the family, when parents are partners in their children's education, the results can be improved student achievement, better school attendance, reduced dropout rates, and decreased delinquency (Riley, 1994).

The review of literature identified barriers to parental involvement and revealed that minority or low-income parents are often underrepresented among the ranks of parents involved with the schools. Although reaching out to parents may seem difficult, the research suggests that most obstacles can be overcome when parents are involved in the education process, a climate for participation is created, and partnerships are formed. Districts must embrace the diversity of families and communities.

National and local research as well as theories and frameworks can help communities identify strengths and weaknesses in parent partnership programs that enable or hinder partnerships. In the current study, Epstein's theory of overlapping spheres of influence and types of parent involvement provided the foundation for family and school partnership activities in the selected school district. It provided the overarching theoretical framework for the study. The separate influences perspective described by Connors and Epstein (1995) views the family and school as having separate roles in influencing the development and education of children.

REFERENCES

Adams, K. S., & Christenson, S. L. (2000). Trust and the family-school relationships: Examination of parent-teacher differences in elementary and secondary grades. *Journal of School Psychology, 38(5),* 477-497.

Anderson, E. S. (1991). *Testing a model of school learning: What contributes to the academic success of at-risk school students?* Unpublished doctoral dissertation, Virginia Polytechnic Insti-tute & State University, Blacksburg

Aspiau, G., Bauer, S. C., & Spillett, M. (1998). Improving the academic performance of Hispanic youth: A community education model. *Bilingual Research Journal,* 22(2), 1-20.

Babbie, E. R. (1990). *Survey research methods* (2nd ed.). Belmont, CA: Wadsworth.

Babbie, E. (1998). *The practice of social research* (8th ed.). Boone, B. J.W. (2002). *A study of parent involvement in Ohio's partnership schools.* Unpublished doctoral dissertation, The Ohio State University, Columbus.

Barclay, K., & Boone, K. (1997). Inviting parents to join in the educational process: What research tells us about parent involvement. *Community Education Journal,* 24, 16-18.

Beecher, R. M. (1984). *Parental involvement: A review of research and principles of successful practice.* Urbana, IL: ERIC Clear-inghouse on Elementary and Early Childhood Education. (ERIC Document Reproduction Service No. ED247032)

Berger, E. (1991). Parent involvement: Yesterday and today. *Elementary School Journal,* 91, 209-218.

Bermudez, A. B., & Marquez, J. A. (1996). An examination of a four-way collaborative to increase parent involvement in the schools. *Journal of Educational Issues of Language Minority Students,* 16, 1-16.

Bogden, R. C., & Biklen, S. K. (1992). *Qualitative research for education: An introduction to theory and methods.* Boston: Allyn and Bacon.

Boone, B. J. W. (2002). *A study of parent involvement in Ohio's partnership schools.* Unpublished doctoral dissertation, The Ohio State University, Columbus.

Bowen, L. A. (2003). *Family school partnerships in Rhode Island suburban middle schools.* Unpublished doctoral dissertation. Johnson & Wales University, Providence, RI.

Bright, J. A. (1996). Partners: An urban black community's perspective on the school and home working together. *New Schools, New Communities,* 12(3), 32-37.

Brim, O. (1965). *Education for child rearing.* New York: Free Press.

Canter, L., & Canter, M. (1991). *Parents on your side.* Santa Monica, CA: Canter and Associates.

Carrasquillo, A., & London, C. B. G. (1993). *Parents and schools: A source book.* Hamden, CT: Garland Publishing.

Chavkin, N. F. (1993). *Families and schools in a pluralistic society.* Albany, NY: State University of New York.

Chavkin, N. F., & Williams, D. L. (1988). Critical issues in teacher training for parent involvement. *Educational Horizons,* 66, 83-86.

Chrispeels, J. H., & Rivero, E. (2000, April). *Engaging Latino families for student success: Understanding the process and impact of providing training to parents.* Paper presented at the meeting of the American Educational Research Association, New Orleans, LA.

Cibulka, J. G., & Kritek, W. J. (Eds.). (1996). *Coordination among schools, families, and communities: Prospects for educational reform.* Albany, NY: State University of New York.

Coleman, J. S., Campbell, E. Q., Hobson, C. J., McPartland, J., Mood, A. M., Weinfield, F. D., et al. (1966). *Equality of educational opportunity.* Washington, DC: National Center for Educational Statistics.

Comer, J. P. (1989). Racism and the education of young children. *Teachers College Record,* 90(3), 352-361.

Connors, L. J., & Epstein, J. L. (1994). *Taking stock: The views of teachers, parents, and students on school, family, and community partnerships in high schools* (No. 25). Baltimore: Johns Hopkins University, Center on Families, Communities, Schools, and Children's Learning.

Connors, L. J., & Epstein, J. L. (1995). Parent and school partnerships. In M. H. Bornstein (Ed.), *Handbook of parenting, volume 4: Applied and practical parenting* (pp. 437-458). Mahwah, NJ: Erlbaum.

Crowley, E. P. (1995). Using qualitative methods in special education research. *Exceptionality,* 5(2), 55-69.

Dauber, S. L., & Epstein, J. L. (1989). *Parents' attitudes and practices of involvement in elementary and middle schools* (CREM Rep. 33). Baltimore: Johns Hopkins University, Center for Research on Elementary and Middle Schools.

Dauber, S. L., & Epstein, J. L. (1993). Parents' attitudes and practices of involvement in inner-city elementary and middle schools. In N. Chavkin (Ed.), *Families and schools in a pluralistic society* (pp. 53-71). Albany, NY: SUNY Press.

Davies, D. (1987). Parent involvement in the public schools. *Education and Urban Society,* 19, 147-163.

Davis, D. (2000). *Supporting parent, family, and community involvement in your school.* Retrieved June 27, 2004, from http://www.nwrel.org

Delgado-Gaitan, C. (1991). Involving parents in the schools: A process of empowerment. *American Journal of Education,* 100(1), 20-46.

Eccles, J. S., & Harold, R. D. (1996). Family involvement in children's and adolescents' schooling. In A. Booth & J. F. Dunn (Eds.), *Family-school links: How do they affect educational outcomes?* (pp. 3-34). Mahwah, NJ: Lawrence Erlbaum Associates.

Eisner, E. W. (1998). *The enlightened eye: Qualitative inquiry and the enhancement of educational practice* (2nd ed.). Upper Saddle River, NJ: Prentice-Hall, Inc.

Epstein, J. (1982). *Student reaction to teacher practices of parent involvement* (No. P-21). Baltimore: Johns Hopkins University, Center for Research on Elementary and Middle Schools.

Epstein, J. (1985). Home and school connections in schools of the future: Implications of research on parent involvement. *Peabody Journal of Education,* 62(2), 18-41.

Epstein, J. L. (1990). School and family connections: Theory, research and implications for integrating sociologies of education and family. In D. Unger & M. Sussman (Eds.), *Families in community settings: Interdisciplinary perspective* (pp. 99-126). New York: Hawort Press.

Epstein, J. L. (1991). Effects of teacher practices of parent involvement on change in student achievement in reading and math. In S. B. Silvern (Ed.), *Advances in reading/language research: Literacy through family, community, and school interaction* (pp. 261-276). Greenwich, CT: JAI Press.

Epstein, J. L. (1992). *School and family partnerships* (Rep. No. 6). Baltimore: Johns Hopkins University, Center on School, Family, and Community Partnerships.

Epstein, J. L. (1995). School/family/community partnerships: Caring for the children we share. *Phi Delta Kappan,* 76(9), 701-712.

Epstein, J. L. (1996). Perspectives and previews on research and policy for school, family, and community partnerships. In A.Booth & J. F. Dunn (Eds.), *Family-school links: How do they affect educational outcomes?* (pp. 209-246). Mahwah, NJ: Erlbaum.

Epstein, J. L., & Dauber, S. (1991). School programs and teacher practices of parent involvement in inner-city elementary and middle schools. *Elementary School Journal,* 91, 289-302.

Epstein, J. L., Coates, L., Salinas, K. C., Sanders, M. G., & Simon, B.S. (1997). *School, family, and community partnerships: Your handbook for action.* Thousand Oaks, CA: Corwin Press.

Evans-Schilling, D. (1996). Preparing educators for family involvement: Reflections, research, and renewal. *Educational Forum,* 51, 35-46.

Finn, J. D. (1998). Parental engagement that makes a difference. *Educational Leadership,* 55(8), 20-24.

Finney, P. (1993, May 17). The PTA/Newsweek national educa tion survey. *Newsweek Magazine.*

Froebel, F. (1887). *The education of man: Education series.* New York: Appleton.

Gariulo, R. M., & Graves, S. B. (1991). Parent feelings. *Childhood Education,* 67(3), 176-178.

Gartrell-Nadine, P. (1995). *Race and parental involvement in school: Restructuring contested terrain.* Unpublished doctoral dissertation, University of California, Berkeley.

Glesne, C., & Peshkin, A. (1992). *Becoming qualitative researchers: An introduction.* White Plains, NY: Longman.

Goals 2000: Educate America Act, Sen. Rep. 103-85, 103d Cong., 1st Sess. (1993).

Gordon, I. J. (1977). Parent education and parental involvement: Retrospect and prospect. *Childhood Education,* 54(2), 71-78.

Gordon, I. J., & Breivogel, W. F. (1976). *Building effective home-school relations.* Boston: Allyn & Bacon.

Greene, J. C., Caracelli, V. J., & Graham, W. F. (1989). Toward a conceptual framework for mixed-method evaluation de sign. *Educational Evaluation and Policy Analysis,* 11(3), 255-274.

Greenwood, G. E., & Hickman, C. W. (1991). Research and practice in parent involvement: Implications for teacher education. *Elementary School Journal,* 91(3), 279-288.

Gruenberg, B. (1927). *Outlines for child study: A manual for parents and teachers.* Columbus, OH: Merrill.

Hamilton-Lee, M. (1988). *Home-school partnerships: The school development program model.* (ERIC Document Reproduction Service No. ED303923)

Haynes, N. M., & Ben-Avie, M. (1996). Parents as full partners in education. In A. Booth & J. F. Dunn (Eds.), *Family-school links: How do they affect educational outcomes?* (pp. 45-55).

Henderson, A. T. (1987). *The evidence continues to grow: Parent involvement improves student achievement.* Columbia, MD: National Committee for Citizens in Education.

Henderson, A. T., & Berla, N. (Eds.). (1994). *A new generation of evidence: The family is critical to student achievement.* Washington, DC: National Committee for Citizens in Education.

Hill, E. J. G. (2003). *Strengthening the link between home and school.* Unpublished doctoral dissertation. University of Southern Mississippi, Hattiesburg.

Hoover-Dempsey, K. V., & Sandler, H. M. (1997). Why do parents become involved in their children's education? *Review of Educational Research, 67*(1), 3-42.

Inger, M. (1992). *Increasing the involvement of Hispanic parents.* New York: ERIC Clearinghouse on Urban Education. (ERIC Document Reproduction Service No. ED350380)

Isaac, S., & Mitchell, W. B. (1995). *Handbook in educational research and evaluation: A collection of principles, methods, and strategies useful in the planning, design, and evaluation of studies in education and the behavioral sciences* (3rd ed.). San Diego, CA: EdITS.

Izzo, C. V., Weissberg, R. P., Kasprow, W. J., & Fendrich, M. (1999). A longitudinal assessment of teacher perceptions of parent inolvement in children's education and school performance. *American Journal of Community Psychology, 27*(6), 817-839.

Jennings, J. (1995). *National issues in education: Goals 2000 and from school to work.* Bloomington, IN: Phi Delta Kappa.

Jordan, C, Orozco, E., & Averett, A. (2001). *Emerging issues in school, family, and community connections.* Austin, TX: National Center for Family and Community Connections with Schools.

Keith, T. Z., Keith, P. B., Troutman, G. C., Bickley, P. G., Trivette, P.S., & Singh, K. (1993). Does parental involvement affect eighth-grade student achievement? Structural analysis of national data. *School Psychology Review,* 22, 474-494.

Keith, T. Z., Reimers, T. M., Fehrman, P. G., Pottebaum, S. M., & Aubrey, L. W. (1986). Parental involvement, homework, and tv time: Direct and indirect effects on high school achievement. *Journal of Educational Psychology,* 76, 373-380.

Kohl, G. O., Lengua, L. J., & McMahon, R. J. (2000). Parent involvement in school conceptualizing multiple dimensions and their relations with family and demographic risk factors. *Journal of School Psychology,* 38(6), 501-523.

Lewis, A. E., & Foreman, T. A. (2002). Contestation or collaboration? A comparative study of home-school relations. *Anthropology and Education Quarterly,* 33(1), 60-89.

Lewis, A. C., & Henderson, A T. (1997). *Urgent message: Families crucial to school reform.* Washington, DC: Center for Law and Education.

Lomotey, K. (1989). Cultural diversity in the school: Implications for principals. *NASSP Bulletin,* 73(521), 81-88.

Maykut, P., & Morehouse, R. (1994). *Beginning qualitative research: A philosophic and practical guide.* Washington, DC: Falmer Press.

Moles, O. C. (1982). Synthesis of recent research on parent

participation in children's education. *Educational Leadership*, 40, 44-47.

Moles, O. C., & D'Angelo, D. (1993). *Building school-family partnerships for learning: Workshops for urban educators.* Washington, DC: Office of Educational Research and Improvement.

Morgan, D. L. (1997). *Focus groups as qualitative research* (2nd ed.). Thousand Oaks, CA: Sage.

Mosteller, F., & Moynihan, D. P. (1972). *On equality of educational opportunity.* New York: Random House.

National Education Goals Panel. (1994). *The national education goals report.* Washington, DC: U.S. Government Printing Office.

National PTA. (1998). *National standards for parent/family involvement programs.* Chicago, IL: Author.

Natriello, G., & McDill, E. L. (1986). Performance standards, student effort on homework, and academic achievement. *Sociology of Education,* 59, 18-31.

No Child Left Behind Act of 2001, Pub. L. No. 107-110, 115 Stat. 1425 (2002).

Orlich, D. C. (1978). *Designing sensible surveys.* Pleasantville, NY: Redgrave Publishing Company.

Parkay, F. W., & Stanford, B. H. (Eds.) (1992). *Becoming a teacher: Accepting the challenge of a profession* (2nd ed.). Allyn & Bacon.

Patton, M. Q. (1990). *Qualitative evaluation and research methods* (2nd ed.). Newburg Park, CA: Sage.

Pestalozzi, L. H. (1915). *How Gertrude teaches her children.* London: Allen & Upwin.

Pratt, D. (1994). *Curriculum planning: A handbook for professionals.* Fort Worth, TX: Harcourt Brace.

Rea, L. M., & Parker, R. A. (1992). *Designing and conducting survey research: A comprehensive guide.* San Francisco: Jossey-Bass.

Rioux, J., & Berla, N. (1993). *Innovations in parent and family involvement.* Princeton, NJ: Eye on Education.

Roehlkepartain, E. C., & Benson, P. L. (1994, October). Connecting schools and families. *Search Institute Source Newsletter*, 1-3.

Rumberger, R. W. (1990). Family influences on dropout behavior in one California high school. *Sociology of Education,* 63(4), 283-299.

Russek, B. E., & Weinberg, S. L. (1993). Mixed methods in a study of implementation of technology-based materials in the elementary classroom. *Evaluation and Program Planning,* 16(2), 131-142.

Sanders, M. (1998). The effects of school, family, and community support on the academic achievement of African-American adolescents. *Urban Education,* 33(3), 385-409.

Scribner, J. D., Young, M. D., & Pedroza, A. (1999). Building collaborative relationships with parents. In P. Reyes, J. D. Scribner, & A. Paredes-Scribner (Eds.), *Lessons from high-performing Hispanic schools: Creating learning communities* (pp. 36-60). New York: Teachers College Press.

Shaver, A. V., & Walls, R. T. (1998). Effect of Title I parent involvement on student reading and mathematics achievement. *Journal of Research and Development in Education,* 31(2), 90-97.

Singh, K. B., Trivette, P. G., Keith, P., & Keith, T. Z. (1995). The effects of four components of parental involvement on eighthgrade student achievement: Structural analysis of NELS-88 data. School *Psychology Review,* 24(2), 299-317.

South Eastern Regional Vision for Education, U.S. Department of Education, Office of Educational Research and Improvement, Educational Resources Information Center. (1996). *Families and schools: An essential partnership.* Washington, DC: Author.

Strauss, A., & Corbin, J. (1990). *Basics of qualitative research: Grounded theory procedures and techniques.* Newbury Park, CA: Sage.

Sui-Chu, E. H., & Willms, J. D. (1996). Effects of parental involvement on eighth-grade achievement. *Sociology of Edu cation, 69*(2), 126-141.

Swap, S. (1990). *Schools reaching out and success for all children: Two case studies.* Boston: Institute for Responsive Education.

Tacq, J. (1997). *Multivariate analysis techniques in social science research: From problem to analysis.* London: Sage Publications

Thornburg, K. (1991). Youth at risk: Society at risk. *Elementary School Journal,* 91(3), 199-207.

Uguroglu, M. E., & Walberg, H. J. (1986). Predicting achieve ment and motivation. *Journal of Research and Development in Education,* 19(3), 1-11.

U.S. Department of Education. (1994). *Strong families, strong schools: Building community partnerships for learning.* Washington, DC: Author.

Vandergrift, J., & Greene, M. E. (1992). Rethinking parent involvement. *Educational Leadership,* 50(1), 57-59.

Walberg, H. J. (1984). Improving the productivity of America's schools. *Educational Leadership,* 41(8), 19-30.

Wang, M. C., Haertel, G. D., & Walberg, H. J. (1993). Toward a knowledge base for school learning. *Review of Educational Research, 63*(3), 249-294.

Whipple, J. (1929). *The twenty-eighth yearbook: National Society for the Study of Education. Preschool and parent education.* Bloomington, IN: Public School Publishing.